THIS BOOK BELONGS TO :

_____

_____

WEEK AT A GLANCE

	MONDAY	TUESDAY	WEDNESDAY	THURSDAY	FRIDAY
GROUP :					
GROUP :					
GROUP :					
GROUP :					
GROUP :					

WEEK AT A GLANCE

	MONDAY	TUESDAY	WEDNESDAY	THURSDAY	FRIDAY
GROUP :					
GROUP :					
GROUP :					
GROUP :					
GROUP :					

WEEK AT A GLANCE

	MONDAY	TUESDAY	WEDNESDAY	THURSDAY	FRIDAY
✎ GROUP :					
✎ GROUP :					
✎ GROUP :					
✎ GROUP :					
✎ GROUP :					

WEEK AT A GLANCE

	MONDAY	TUESDAY	WEDNESDAY	THURSDAY	FRIDAY
✏ GROUP :					
✏ GROUP :					
✏ GROUP :					
✏ GROUP :					
✏ GROUP :					

WEEK AT A GLANCE

	MONDAY	TUESDAY	WEDNESDAY	THURSDAY	FRIDAY
✎ GROUP :					
✎ GROUP :					
✎ GROUP :					
✎ GROUP :					
✎ GROUP :					

WEEK AT A GLANCE

	MONDAY	TUESDAY	WEDNESDAY	THURSDAY	FRIDAY
GROUP :					
GROUP :					
GROUP :					
GROUP :					
GROUP :					

WEEK AT A GLANCE

	MONDAY	TUESDAY	WEDNESDAY	THURSDAY	FRIDAY
GROUP :					
GROUP :					
GROUP :					
GROUP :					
GROUP :					

WEEK AT A GLANCE

	MONDAY	TUESDAY	WEDNESDAY	THURSDAY	FRIDAY
✏ GROUP :					
✏ GROUP :					
✏ GROUP :					
✏ GROUP :					
✏ GROUP :					

WEEK AT A GLANCE

	MONDAY	TUESDAY	WEDNESDAY	THURSDAY	FRIDAY
GROUP :					
GROUP :					
GROUP :					
GROUP :					
GROUP :					

WEEK AT A GLANCE

	MONDAY	TUESDAY	WEDNESDAY	THURSDAY	FRIDAY
✏ GROUP :					
✏ GROUP :					
✏ GROUP :					
✏ GROUP :					
✏ GROUP :					

WEEK AT A GLANCE

	MONDAY	TUESDAY	WEDNESDAY	THURSDAY	FRIDAY
✎ GROUP :					
✎ GROUP :					
✎ GROUP :					
✎ GROUP :					
✎ GROUP :					

WEEK AT A GLANCE

	MONDAY	TUESDAY	WEDNESDAY	THURSDAY	FRIDAY
✏ GROUP :					
✏ GROUP :					
✏ GROUP :					
✏ GROUP :					
✏ GROUP :					

WEEK AT A GLANCE

	MONDAY	TUESDAY	WEDNESDAY	THURSDAY	FRIDAY
GROUP :					
GROUP :					
GROUP :					
GROUP :					
GROUP :					

WEEK AT A GLANCE

	MONDAY	TUESDAY	WEDNESDAY	THURSDAY	FRIDAY
✏ GROUP :					
✏ GROUP :					
✏ GROUP :					
✏ GROUP :					
✏ GROUP :					

WEEK AT A GLANCE

	MONDAY	TUESDAY	WEDNESDAY	THURSDAY	FRIDAY
✏ GROUP :					
✏ GROUP :					
✏ GROUP :					
✏ GROUP :					
✏ GROUP :					

WEEK AT A GLANCE

	MONDAY	TUESDAY	WEDNESDAY	THURSDAY	FRIDAY
GROUP :					
GROUP :					
GROUP :					
GROUP :					
GROUP :					

WEEK AT A GLANCE

	MONDAY	TUESDAY	WEDNESDAY	THURSDAY	FRIDAY
✏ GROUP :					
✏ GROUP :					
✏ GROUP :					
✏ GROUP :					
✏ GROUP :					

WEEK AT A GLANCE

	MONDAY	TUESDAY	WEDNESDAY	THURSDAY	FRIDAY
✏ GROUP :					
✏ GROUP :					
✏ GROUP :					
✏ GROUP :					
✏ GROUP :					

WEEK AT A GLANCE

	MONDAY	TUESDAY	WEDNESDAY	THURSDAY	FRIDAY
GROUP :					
GROUP :					
GROUP :					
GROUP :					
GROUP :					

WEEK AT A GLANCE

	MONDAY	TUESDAY	WEDNESDAY	THURSDAY	FRIDAY
✏ GROUP :					
✏ GROUP :					
✏ GROUP :					
✏ GROUP :					
✏ GROUP :					

GUIDED READING PLANBOOK

GROUP : DATE :

BOOK TITLE : LEVEL :

✎ BOOK INTRODUCTION :

✎ WORD WORK : ✎ VOCABULARY :

✎ TEACHING POINT / STRATEGY :

✎ BEFORE READING :

✎ DURING READING :

✎ AFTER READING :

✎ NOTES :

GUIDED READING OBSERVATION NOTES

STUDENT:		
AFTER READING	Makes predictions	
	Notices new words	
	Recognises sight words	
	Scans text for clues	
	Scans images for clues	
DURING READING	Applies strategies for new words	
	Reads fluently	
	Self-corrects	
	Re-reads for meaning	
BEFORE READING	Identifies main ideas	
	Summarizes topic in one sentence	
	Recalls events in proper order	
	Retells text accurately	

Notes:

STUDENT:		
AFTER READING	Makes predictions	
	Notices new words	
	Recognises sight words	
	Scans text for clues	
	Scans images for clues	
DURING READING	Applies strategies for new words	
	Reads fluently	
	Self-corrects	
	Re-reads for meaning	
BEFORE READING	Identifies main ideas	
	Summarizes topic in one sentence	
	Recalls events in proper order	
	Retells text accurately	

Notes:

STUDENT:		
AFTER READING	Makes predictions	
	Notices new words	
	Recognises sight words	
	Scans text for clues	
	Scans images for clues	
DURING READING	Applies strategies for new words	
	Reads fluently	
	Self-corrects	
	Re-reads for meaning	
BEFORE READING	Identifies main ideas	
	Summarizes topic in one sentence	
	Recalls events in proper order	
	Retells text accurately	

Notes:

STUDENT:		
AFTER READING	Makes predictions	
	Notices new words	
	Recognises sight words	
	Scans text for clues	
	Scans images for clues	
DURING READING	Applies strategies for new words	
	Reads fluently	
	Self-corrects	
	Re-reads for meaning	
BEFORE READING	Identifies main ideas	
	Summarizes topic in one sentence	
	Recalls events in proper order	
	Retells text accurately	

Notes:

STUDENT:		
AFTER READING	Makes predictions	
	Notices new words	
	Recognises sight words	
	Scans text for clues	
	Scans images for clues	
DURING READING	Applies strategies for new words	
	Reads fluently	
	Self-corrects	
	Re-reads for meaning	
BEFORE READING	Identifies main ideas	
	Summarizes topic in one sentence	
	Recalls events in proper order	
	Retells text accurately	

Notes:

STUDENT:		
AFTER READING	Makes predictions	
	Notices new words	
	Recognises sight words	
	Scans text for clues	
	Scans images for clues	
DURING READING	Applies strategies for new words	
	Reads fluently	
	Self-corrects	
	Re-reads for meaning	
BEFORE READING	Identifies main ideas	
	Summarizes topic in one sentence	
	Recalls events in proper order	
	Retells text accurately	

Notes:

GUIDED READING PLANBOOK

GROUP :   DATE :

BOOK TITLE :   LEVEL :

✎ BOOK INTRODUCTION :

✎ WORD WORK :   ✎ VOCABULARY :

✎ TEACHING POINT / STRATEGY :

✎ BEFORE READING :

✎ DURING READING :

✎ AFTER READING :

✎ NOTES :

GUIDED READING OBSERVATION NOTES

STUDENT :		
AFTER READING	Makes predictions	
	Notices new words	
	Recognises sight words	
	Scans text for clues	
	Scans images for clues	
DURING READING	Applies strategies for new words	
	Reads fluently	
	Self-corrects	
	Re-reads for meaning	
BEFORE READING	Identifies main ideas	
	Summarizes topic in one sentence	
	Recalls events in proper order	
	Retells text accurately	

Notes :

STUDENT :		
AFTER READING	Makes predictions	
	Notices new words	
	Recognises sight words	
	Scans text for clues	
	Scans images for clues	
DURING READING	Applies strategies for new words	
	Reads fluently	
	Self-corrects	
	Re-reads for meaning	
BEFORE READING	Identifies main ideas	
	Summarizes topic in one sentence	
	Recalls events in proper order	
	Retells text accurately	

Notes :

STUDENT :		
AFTER READING	Makes predictions	
	Notices new words	
	Recognises sight words	
	Scans text for clues	
	Scans images for clues	
DURING READING	Applies strategies for new words	
	Reads fluently	
	Self-corrects	
	Re-reads for meaning	
BEFORE READING	Identifies main ideas	
	Summarizes topic in one sentence	
	Recalls events in proper order	
	Retells text accurately	

Notes :

STUDENT :		
AFTER READING	Makes predictions	
	Notices new words	
	Recognises sight words	
	Scans text for clues	
	Scans images for clues	
DURING READING	Applies strategies for new words	
	Reads fluently	
	Self-corrects	
	Re-reads for meaning	
BEFORE READING	Identifies main ideas	
	Summarizes topic in one sentence	
	Recalls events in proper order	
	Retells text accurately	

Notes :

STUDENT :		
AFTER READING	Makes predictions	
	Notices new words	
	Recognises sight words	
	Scans text for clues	
	Scans images for clues	
DURING READING	Applies strategies for new words	
	Reads fluently	
	Self-corrects	
	Re-reads for meaning	
BEFORE READING	Identifies main ideas	
	Summarizes topic in one sentence	
	Recalls events in proper order	
	Retells text accurately	

Notes :

STUDENT :		
AFTER READING	Makes predictions	
	Notices new words	
	Recognises sight words	
	Scans text for clues	
	Scans images for clues	
DURING READING	Applies strategies for new words	
	Reads fluently	
	Self-corrects	
	Re-reads for meaning	
BEFORE READING	Identifies main ideas	
	Summarizes topic in one sentence	
	Recalls events in proper order	
	Retells text accurately	

Notes :

GUIDED READING PLANBOOK

GROUP :   DATE :

BOOK TITLE :   LEVEL :

✎ BOOK INTRODUCTION :

✎ WORD WORK :   ✎ VOCABULARY :

✎ TEACHING POINT / STRATEGY :

✎ BEFORE READING :

✎ DURING READING :

✎ AFTER READING :

✎ NOTES :

GUIDED READING OBSERVATION NOTES

	STUDENT :	
AFTER READING	Makes predictions	
	Notices new words	
	Recognises sight words	
	Scans text for clues	
	Scans images for clues	
DURING READING	Applies strategies for new words	
	Reads fluently	
	Self-corrects	
	Re-reads for meaning	
BEFORE READING	Identifies main ideas	
	Summarizes topic in one sentence	
	Recalls events in proper order	
	Retells text accurately	

Notes :

	STUDENT :	
AFTER READING	Makes predictions	
	Notices new words	
	Recognises sight words	
	Scans text for clues	
	Scans images for clues	
DURING READING	Applies strategies for new words	
	Reads fluently	
	Self-corrects	
	Re-reads for meaning	
BEFORE READING	Identifies main ideas	
	Summarizes topic in one sentence	
	Recalls events in proper order	
	Retells text accurately	

Notes :

	STUDENT :	
AFTER READING	Makes predictions	
	Notices new words	
	Recognises sight words	
	Scans text for clues	
	Scans images for clues	
DURING READING	Applies strategies for new words	
	Reads fluently	
	Self-corrects	
	Re-reads for meaning	
BEFORE READING	Identifies main ideas	
	Summarizes topic in one sentence	
	Recalls events in proper order	
	Retells text accurately	

Notes :

	STUDENT :	
AFTER READING	Makes predictions	
	Notices new words	
	Recognises sight words	
	Scans text for clues	
	Scans images for clues	
DURING READING	Applies strategies for new words	
	Reads fluently	
	Self-corrects	
	Re-reads for meaning	
BEFORE READING	Identifies main ideas	
	Summarizes topic in one sentence	
	Recalls events in proper order	
	Retells text accurately	

Notes :

	STUDENT :	
AFTER READING	Makes predictions	
	Notices new words	
	Recognises sight words	
	Scans text for clues	
	Scans images for clues	
DURING READING	Applies strategies for new words	
	Reads fluently	
	Self-corrects	
	Re-reads for meaning	
BEFORE READING	Identifies main ideas	
	Summarizes topic in one sentence	
	Recalls events in proper order	
	Retells text accurately	

Notes :

	STUDENT :	
AFTER READING	Makes predictions	
	Notices new words	
	Recognises sight words	
	Scans text for clues	
	Scans images for clues	
DURING READING	Applies strategies for new words	
	Reads fluently	
	Self-corrects	
	Re-reads for meaning	
BEFORE READING	Identifies main ideas	
	Summarizes topic in one sentence	
	Recalls events in proper order	
	Retells text accurately	

Notes :

GUIDED READING PLANBOOK

GROUP : DATE :
BOOK TITLE : LEVEL :

✏ BOOK INTRODUCTION :

✏ WORD WORK :

✏ VOCABULARY :

✏ TEACHING POINT / STRATEGY :

✏ BEFORE READING :

✏ DURING READING :

✏ AFTER READING :

✏ NOTES :

GUIDED READING OBSERVATION NOTES

STUDENT :

AFTER READING	Makes predictions	
	Notices new words	
	Recognises sight words	
	Scans text for clues	
	Scans images for clues	
DURING READING	Applies strategies for new words	
	Reads fluently	
	Self-corrects	
	Re-reads for meaning	
BEFORE READING	Identifies main ideas	
	Summarizes topic in one sentence	
	Recalls events in proper order	
	Retells text accurately	

Notes :

STUDENT :

AFTER READING	Makes predictions	
	Notices new words	
	Recognises sight words	
	Scans text for clues	
	Scans images for clues	
DURING READING	Applies strategies for new words	
	Reads fluently	
	Self-corrects	
	Re-reads for meaning	
BEFORE READING	Identifies main ideas	
	Summarizes topic in one sentence	
	Recalls events in proper order	
	Retells text accurately	

Notes :

STUDENT :

AFTER READING	Makes predictions	
	Notices new words	
	Recognises sight words	
	Scans text for clues	
	Scans images for clues	
DURING READING	Applies strategies for new words	
	Reads fluently	
	Self-corrects	
	Re-reads for meaning	
BEFORE READING	Identifies main ideas	
	Summarizes topic in one sentence	
	Recalls events in proper order	
	Retells text accurately	

Notes :

STUDENT :

AFTER READING	Makes predictions	
	Notices new words	
	Recognises sight words	
	Scans text for clues	
	Scans images for clues	
DURING READING	Applies strategies for new words	
	Reads fluently	
	Self-corrects	
	Re-reads for meaning	
BEFORE READING	Identifies main ideas	
	Summarizes topic in one sentence	
	Recalls events in proper order	
	Retells text accurately	

Notes :

STUDENT :

AFTER READING	Makes predictions	
	Notices new words	
	Recognises sight words	
	Scans text for clues	
	Scans images for clues	
DURING READING	Applies strategies for new words	
	Reads fluently	
	Self-corrects	
	Re-reads for meaning	
BEFORE READING	Identifies main ideas	
	Summarizes topic in one sentence	
	Recalls events in proper order	
	Retells text accurately	

Notes :

STUDENT :

AFTER READING	Makes predictions	
	Notices new words	
	Recognises sight words	
	Scans text for clues	
	Scans images for clues	
DURING READING	Applies strategies for new words	
	Reads fluently	
	Self-corrects	
	Re-reads for meaning	
BEFORE READING	Identifies main ideas	
	Summarizes topic in one sentence	
	Recalls events in proper order	
	Retells text accurately	

Notes :

GUIDED READING PLANBOOK

GROUP :

DATE :

BOOK TITLE :

LEVEL :

✏ BOOK INTRODUCTION :

✏ WORD WORK :

✏ VOCABULARY :

✏ TEACHING POINT / STRATEGY :

✏ BEFORE READING :

✏ DURING READING :

✏ AFTER READING :

✏ NOTES :

GUIDED READING OBSERVATION NOTES

	STUDENT :	
AFTER READING	Makes predictions	
	Notices new words	
	Recognises sight words	
	Scans text for clues	
	Scans images for clues	
DURING READING	Applies strategies for new words	
	Reads fluently	
	Self-corrects	
	Re-reads for meaning	
BEFORE READING	Identifies main ideas	
	Summarizes topic in one sentence	
	Recalls events in proper order	
	Retells text accurately	

Notes :

	STUDENT :	
AFTER READING	Makes predictions	
	Notices new words	
	Recognises sight words	
	Scans text for clues	
	Scans images for clues	
DURING READING	Applies strategies for new words	
	Reads fluently	
	Self-corrects	
	Re-reads for meaning	
BEFORE READING	Identifies main ideas	
	Summarizes topic in one sentence	
	Recalls events in proper order	
	Retells text accurately	

Notes :

	STUDENT :	
AFTER READING	Makes predictions	
	Notices new words	
	Recognises sight words	
	Scans text for clues	
	Scans images for clues	
DURING READING	Applies strategies for new words	
	Reads fluently	
	Self-corrects	
	Re-reads for meaning	
BEFORE READING	Identifies main ideas	
	Summarizes topic in one sentence	
	Recalls events in proper order	
	Retells text accurately	

Notes :

	STUDENT :	
AFTER READING	Makes predictions	
	Notices new words	
	Recognises sight words	
	Scans text for clues	
	Scans images for clues	
DURING READING	Applies strategies for new words	
	Reads fluently	
	Self-corrects	
	Re-reads for meaning	
BEFORE READING	Identifies main ideas	
	Summarizes topic in one sentence	
	Recalls events in proper order	
	Retells text accurately	

Notes :

	STUDENT :	
AFTER READING	Makes predictions	
	Notices new words	
	Recognises sight words	
	Scans text for clues	
	Scans images for clues	
DURING READING	Applies strategies for new words	
	Reads fluently	
	Self-corrects	
	Re-reads for meaning	
BEFORE READING	Identifies main ideas	
	Summarizes topic in one sentence	
	Recalls events in proper order	
	Retells text accurately	

Notes :

	STUDENT :	
AFTER READING	Makes predictions	
	Notices new words	
	Recognises sight words	
	Scans text for clues	
	Scans images for clues	
DURING READING	Applies strategies for new words	
	Reads fluently	
	Self-corrects	
	Re-reads for meaning	
BEFORE READING	Identifies main ideas	
	Summarizes topic in one sentence	
	Recalls events in proper order	
	Retells text accurately	

Notes :

GUIDED READING PLANBOOK

GROUP :   DATE :

BOOK TITLE :   LEVEL :

✏ BOOK INTRODUCTION :

✏ WORD WORK :   ✏ VOCABULARY :

✏ TEACHING POINT / STRATEGY :

✏ BEFORE READING :

✏ DURING READING :

✏ AFTER READING :

✏ NOTES :

GUIDED READING OBSERVATION NOTES

STUDENT :		
AFTER READING	Makes predictions	
	Notices new words	
	Recognises sight words	
	Scans text for clues	
	Scans images for clues	
DURING READING	Applies strategies for new words	
	Reads fluently	
	Self-corrects	
	Re-reads for meaning	
BEFORE READING	Identifies main ideas	
	Summarizes topic in one sentence	
	Recalls events in proper order	
	Retells text accurately	

Notes :

STUDENT :		
AFTER READING	Makes predictions	
	Notices new words	
	Recognises sight words	
	Scans text for clues	
	Scans images for clues	
DURING READING	Applies strategies for new words	
	Reads fluently	
	Self-corrects	
	Re-reads for meaning	
BEFORE READING	Identifies main ideas	
	Summarizes topic in one sentence	
	Recalls events in proper order	
	Retells text accurately	

Notes :

STUDENT :		
AFTER READING	Makes predictions	
	Notices new words	
	Recognises sight words	
	Scans text for clues	
	Scans images for clues	
DURING READING	Applies strategies for new words	
	Reads fluently	
	Self-corrects	
	Re-reads for meaning	
BEFORE READING	Identifies main ideas	
	Summarizes topic in one sentence	
	Recalls events in proper order	
	Retells text accurately	

Notes :

STUDENT :		
AFTER READING	Makes predictions	
	Notices new words	
	Recognises sight words	
	Scans text for clues	
	Scans images for clues	
DURING READING	Applies strategies for new words	
	Reads fluently	
	Self-corrects	
	Re-reads for meaning	
BEFORE READING	Identifies main ideas	
	Summarizes topic in one sentence	
	Recalls events in proper order	
	Retells text accurately	

Notes :

STUDENT :		
AFTER READING	Makes predictions	
	Notices new words	
	Recognises sight words	
	Scans text for clues	
	Scans images for clues	
DURING READING	Applies strategies for new words	
	Reads fluently	
	Self-corrects	
	Re-reads for meaning	
BEFORE READING	Identifies main ideas	
	Summarizes topic in one sentence	
	Recalls events in proper order	
	Retells text accurately	

Notes :

STUDENT :		
AFTER READING	Makes predictions	
	Notices new words	
	Recognises sight words	
	Scans text for clues	
	Scans images for clues	
DURING READING	Applies strategies for new words	
	Reads fluently	
	Self-corrects	
	Re-reads for meaning	
BEFORE READING	Identifies main ideas	
	Summarizes topic in one sentence	
	Recalls events in proper order	
	Retells text accurately	

Notes :

GUIDED READING PLANBOOK

GROUP :

DATE :

BOOK TITLE :

LEVEL :

✎ BOOK INTRODUCTION :

✎ WORD WORK :

✎ VOCABULARY :

✎ TEACHING POINT / STRATEGY :

✎ BEFORE READING :

✎ DURING READING :

✎ AFTER READING :

✎ NOTES :

GUIDED READING OBSERVATION NOTES

STUDENT :		
AFTER READING	Makes predictions	
	Notices new words	
	Recognises sight words	
	Scans text for clues	
	Scans images for clues	
DURING READING	Applies strategies for new words	
	Reads fluently	
	Self-corrects	
	Re-reads for meaning	
BEFORE READING	Identifies main ideas	
	Summarizes topic in one sentence	
	Recalls events in proper order	
	Retells text accurately	

Notes :

STUDENT :		
AFTER READING	Makes predictions	
	Notices new words	
	Recognises sight words	
	Scans text for clues	
	Scans images for clues	
DURING READING	Applies strategies for new words	
	Reads fluently	
	Self-corrects	
	Re-reads for meaning	
BEFORE READING	Identifies main ideas	
	Summarizes topic in one sentence	
	Recalls events in proper order	
	Retells text accurately	

Notes :

STUDENT :		
AFTER READING	Makes predictions	
	Notices new words	
	Recognises sight words	
	Scans text for clues	
	Scans images for clues	
DURING READING	Applies strategies for new words	
	Reads fluently	
	Self-corrects	
	Re-reads for meaning	
BEFORE READING	Identifies main ideas	
	Summarizes topic in one sentence	
	Recalls events in proper order	
	Retells text accurately	

Notes :

STUDENT :		
AFTER READING	Makes predictions	
	Notices new words	
	Recognises sight words	
	Scans text for clues	
	Scans images for clues	
DURING READING	Applies strategies for new words	
	Reads fluently	
	Self-corrects	
	Re-reads for meaning	
BEFORE READING	Identifies main ideas	
	Summarizes topic in one sentence	
	Recalls events in proper order	
	Retells text accurately	

Notes :

STUDENT :		
AFTER READING	Makes predictions	
	Notices new words	
	Recognises sight words	
	Scans text for clues	
	Scans images for clues	
DURING READING	Applies strategies for new words	
	Reads fluently	
	Self-corrects	
	Re-reads for meaning	
BEFORE READING	Identifies main ideas	
	Summarizes topic in one sentence	
	Recalls events in proper order	
	Retells text accurately	

Notes :

STUDENT :		
AFTER READING	Makes predictions	
	Notices new words	
	Recognises sight words	
	Scans text for clues	
	Scans images for clues	
DURING READING	Applies strategies for new words	
	Reads fluently	
	Self-corrects	
	Re-reads for meaning	
BEFORE READING	Identifies main ideas	
	Summarizes topic in one sentence	
	Recalls events in proper order	
	Retells text accurately	

Notes :

GUIDED READING PLANBOOK

GROUP :

DATE :

BOOK TITLE :

LEVEL :

✏ BOOK INTRODUCTION :

✏ WORD WORK :

✏ VOCABULARY :

✏ TEACHING POINT / STRATEGY :

✏ BEFORE READING :

✏ DURING READING :

✏ AFTER READING :

✏ NOTES :

GUIDED READING OBSERVATION NOTES

STUDENT :

AFTER READING	Makes predictions	
	Notices new words	
	Recognises sight words	
	Scans text for clues	
	Scans images for clues	
DURING READING	Applies strategies for new words	
	Reads fluently	
	Self-corrects	
	Re-reads for meaning	
BEFORE READING	Identifies main ideas	
	Summarizes topic in one sentence	
	Recalls events in proper order	
	Retells text accurately	

Notes :

STUDENT :

AFTER READING	Makes predictions	
	Notices new words	
	Recognises sight words	
	Scans text for clues	
	Scans images for clues	
DURING READING	Applies strategies for new words	
	Reads fluently	
	Self-corrects	
	Re-reads for meaning	
BEFORE READING	Identifies main ideas	
	Summarizes topic in one sentence	
	Recalls events in proper order	
	Retells text accurately	

Notes :

STUDENT :

AFTER READING	Makes predictions	
	Notices new words	
	Recognises sight words	
	Scans text for clues	
	Scans images for clues	
DURING READING	Applies strategies for new words	
	Reads fluently	
	Self-corrects	
	Re-reads for meaning	
BEFORE READING	Identifies main ideas	
	Summarizes topic in one sentence	
	Recalls events in proper order	
	Retells text accurately	

Notes :

STUDENT :

AFTER READING	Makes predictions	
	Notices new words	
	Recognises sight words	
	Scans text for clues	
	Scans images for clues	
DURING READING	Applies strategies for new words	
	Reads fluently	
	Self-corrects	
	Re-reads for meaning	
BEFORE READING	Identifies main ideas	
	Summarizes topic in one sentence	
	Recalls events in proper order	
	Retells text accurately	

Notes :

STUDENT :

AFTER READING	Makes predictions	
	Notices new words	
	Recognises sight words	
	Scans text for clues	
	Scans images for clues	
DURING READING	Applies strategies for new words	
	Reads fluently	
	Self-corrects	
	Re-reads for meaning	
BEFORE READING	Identifies main ideas	
	Summarizes topic in one sentence	
	Recalls events in proper order	
	Retells text accurately	

Notes :

STUDENT :

AFTER READING	Makes predictions	
	Notices new words	
	Recognises sight words	
	Scans text for clues	
	Scans images for clues	
DURING READING	Applies strategies for new words	
	Reads fluently	
	Self-corrects	
	Re-reads for meaning	
BEFORE READING	Identifies main ideas	
	Summarizes topic in one sentence	
	Recalls events in proper order	
	Retells text accurately	

Notes :

GUIDED READING PLANBOOK

GROUP :

BOOK TITLE :

DATE :

LEVEL :

✎ BOOK INTRODUCTION :

✎ WORD WORK :

✎ VOCABULARY :

✎ TEACHING POINT / STRATEGY :

✎ BEFORE READING :

✎ DURING READING :

✎ AFTER READING :

✎ NOTES :

GUIDED READING OBSERVATION NOTES

STUDENT :		
AFTER READING	Makes predictions	
	Notices new words	
	Recognises sight words	
	Scans text for clues	
	Scans images for clues	
DURING READING	Applies strategies for new words	
	Reads fluently	
	Self-corrects	
	Re-reads for meaning	
BEFORE READING	Identifies main ideas	
	Summarizes topic in one sentence	
	Recalls events in proper order	
	Retells text accurately	

Notes :

STUDENT :		
AFTER READING	Makes predictions	
	Notices new words	
	Recognises sight words	
	Scans text for clues	
	Scans images for clues	
DURING READING	Applies strategies for new words	
	Reads fluently	
	Self-corrects	
	Re-reads for meaning	
BEFORE READING	Identifies main ideas	
	Summarizes topic in one sentence	
	Recalls events in proper order	
	Retells text accurately	

Notes :

STUDENT :		
AFTER READING	Makes predictions	
	Notices new words	
	Recognises sight words	
	Scans text for clues	
	Scans images for clues	
DURING READING	Applies strategies for new words	
	Reads fluently	
	Self-corrects	
	Re-reads for meaning	
BEFORE READING	Identifies main ideas	
	Summarizes topic in one sentence	
	Recalls events in proper order	
	Retells text accurately	

Notes :

STUDENT :		
AFTER READING	Makes predictions	
	Notices new words	
	Recognises sight words	
	Scans text for clues	
	Scans images for clues	
DURING READING	Applies strategies for new words	
	Reads fluently	
	Self-corrects	
	Re-reads for meaning	
BEFORE READING	Identifies main ideas	
	Summarizes topic in one sentence	
	Recalls events in proper order	
	Retells text accurately	

Notes :

STUDENT :		
AFTER READING	Makes predictions	
	Notices new words	
	Recognises sight words	
	Scans text for clues	
	Scans images for clues	
DURING READING	Applies strategies for new words	
	Reads fluently	
	Self-corrects	
	Re-reads for meaning	
BEFORE READING	Identifies main ideas	
	Summarizes topic in one sentence	
	Recalls events in proper order	
	Retells text accurately	

Notes :

STUDENT :		
AFTER READING	Makes predictions	
	Notices new words	
	Recognises sight words	
	Scans text for clues	
	Scans images for clues	
DURING READING	Applies strategies for new words	
	Reads fluently	
	Self-corrects	
	Re-reads for meaning	
BEFORE READING	Identifies main ideas	
	Summarizes topic in one sentence	
	Recalls events in proper order	
	Retells text accurately	

Notes :

GUIDED READING PLANBOOK

GROUP : DATE :

BOOK TITLE : LEVEL :

✏ BOOK INTRODUCTION :

✏ WORD WORK :

✏ VOCABULARY :

✏ TEACHING POINT / STRATEGY :

✏ BEFORE READING :

✏ DURING READING :

✏ AFTER READING :

✏ NOTES :

GUIDED READING OBSERVATION NOTES

STUDENT :		
AFTER READING	Makes predictions	
	Notices new words	
	Recognises sight words	
	Scans text for clues	
	Scans images for clues	
DURING READING	Applies strategies for new words	
	Reads fluently	
	Self-corrects	
	Re-reads for meaning	
BEFORE READING	Identifies main ideas	
	Summarizes topic in one sentence	
	Recalls events in proper order	
	Retells text accurately	

Notes :

STUDENT :		
AFTER READING	Makes predictions	
	Notices new words	
	Recognises sight words	
	Scans text for clues	
	Scans images for clues	
DURING READING	Applies strategies for new words	
	Reads fluently	
	Self-corrects	
	Re-reads for meaning	
BEFORE READING	Identifies main ideas	
	Summarizes topic in one sentence	
	Recalls events in proper order	
	Retells text accurately	

Notes :

STUDENT :		
AFTER READING	Makes predictions	
	Notices new words	
	Recognises sight words	
	Scans text for clues	
	Scans images for clues	
DURING READING	Applies strategies for new words	
	Reads fluently	
	Self-corrects	
	Re-reads for meaning	
BEFORE READING	Identifies main ideas	
	Summarizes topic in one sentence	
	Recalls events in proper order	
	Retells text accurately	

Notes :

STUDENT :		
AFTER READING	Makes predictions	
	Notices new words	
	Recognises sight words	
	Scans text for clues	
	Scans images for clues	
DURING READING	Applies strategies for new words	
	Reads fluently	
	Self-corrects	
	Re-reads for meaning	
BEFORE READING	Identifies main ideas	
	Summarizes topic in one sentence	
	Recalls events in proper order	
	Retells text accurately	

Notes :

STUDENT :		
AFTER READING	Makes predictions	
	Notices new words	
	Recognises sight words	
	Scans text for clues	
	Scans images for clues	
DURING READING	Applies strategies for new words	
	Reads fluently	
	Self-corrects	
	Re-reads for meaning	
BEFORE READING	Identifies main ideas	
	Summarizes topic in one sentence	
	Recalls events in proper order	
	Retells text accurately	

Notes :

STUDENT :		
AFTER READING	Makes predictions	
	Notices new words	
	Recognises sight words	
	Scans text for clues	
	Scans images for clues	
DURING READING	Applies strategies for new words	
	Reads fluently	
	Self-corrects	
	Re-reads for meaning	
BEFORE READING	Identifies main ideas	
	Summarizes topic in one sentence	
	Recalls events in proper order	
	Retells text accurately	

Notes :

GUIDED READING PLANBOOK

GROUP :   DATE :

BOOK TITLE :   LEVEL :

✏ BOOK INTRODUCTION :

✏ WORD WORK :   ✏ VOCABULARY :

✏ TEACHING POINT / STRATEGY :

✏ BEFORE READING :

✏ DURING READING :

✏ AFTER READING :

✏ NOTES :

GUIDED READING OBSERVATION NOTES

STUDENT :		
AFTER READING	Makes predictions	
	Notices new words	
	Recognises sight words	
	Scans text for clues	
	Scans images for clues	
DURING READING	Applies strategies for new words	
	Reads fluently	
	Self-corrects	
	Re-reads for meaning	
BEFORE READING	Identifies main ideas	
	Summarizes topic in one sentence	
	Recalls events in proper order	
	Retells text accurately	

Notes :

STUDENT :		
AFTER READING	Makes predictions	
	Notices new words	
	Recognises sight words	
	Scans text for clues	
	Scans images for clues	
DURING READING	Applies strategies for new words	
	Reads fluently	
	Self-corrects	
	Re-reads for meaning	
BEFORE READING	Identifies main ideas	
	Summarizes topic in one sentence	
	Recalls events in proper order	
	Retells text accurately	

Notes :

STUDENT :		
AFTER READING	Makes predictions	
	Notices new words	
	Recognises sight words	
	Scans text for clues	
	Scans images for clues	
DURING READING	Applies strategies for new words	
	Reads fluently	
	Self-corrects	
	Re-reads for meaning	
BEFORE READING	Identifies main ideas	
	Summarizes topic in one sentence	
	Recalls events in proper order	
	Retells text accurately	

Notes :

STUDENT :		
AFTER READING	Makes predictions	
	Notices new words	
	Recognises sight words	
	Scans text for clues	
	Scans images for clues	
DURING READING	Applies strategies for new words	
	Reads fluently	
	Self-corrects	
	Re-reads for meaning	
BEFORE READING	Identifies main ideas	
	Summarizes topic in one sentence	
	Recalls events in proper order	
	Retells text accurately	

Notes :

STUDENT :		
AFTER READING	Makes predictions	
	Notices new words	
	Recognises sight words	
	Scans text for clues	
	Scans images for clues	
DURING READING	Applies strategies for new words	
	Reads fluently	
	Self-corrects	
	Re-reads for meaning	
BEFORE READING	Identifies main ideas	
	Summarizes topic in one sentence	
	Recalls events in proper order	
	Retells text accurately	

Notes :

STUDENT :		
AFTER READING	Makes predictions	
	Notices new words	
	Recognises sight words	
	Scans text for clues	
	Scans images for clues	
DURING READING	Applies strategies for new words	
	Reads fluently	
	Self-corrects	
	Re-reads for meaning	
BEFORE READING	Identifies main ideas	
	Summarizes topic in one sentence	
	Recalls events in proper order	
	Retells text accurately	

Notes :

GUIDED READING PLANBOOK

GROUP :   DATE :

BOOK TITLE :   LEVEL :

✏ BOOK INTRODUCTION :

✏ WORD WORK :   ✏ VOCABULARY :

✏ TEACHING POINT / STRATEGY :

✏ BEFORE READING :

✏ DURING READING :

✏ AFTER READING :

✏ NOTES :

GUIDED READING OBSERVATION NOTES

STUDENT :

AFTER READING	Makes predictions	
	Notices new words	
	Recognises sight words	
	Scans text for clues	
	Scans images for clues	
DURING READING	Applies strategies for new words	
	Reads fluently	
	Self-corrects	
	Re-reads for meaning	
BEFORE READING	Identifies main ideas	
	Summarizes topic in one sentence	
	Recalls events in proper order	
	Retells text accurately	

Notes :

STUDENT :

AFTER READING	Makes predictions	
	Notices new words	
	Recognises sight words	
	Scans text for clues	
	Scans images for clues	
DURING READING	Applies strategies for new words	
	Reads fluently	
	Self-corrects	
	Re-reads for meaning	
BEFORE READING	Identifies main ideas	
	Summarizes topic in one sentence	
	Recalls events in proper order	
	Retells text accurately	

Notes :

STUDENT :

AFTER READING	Makes predictions	
	Notices new words	
	Recognises sight words	
	Scans text for clues	
	Scans images for clues	
DURING READING	Applies strategies for new words	
	Reads fluently	
	Self-corrects	
	Re-reads for meaning	
BEFORE READING	Identifies main ideas	
	Summarizes topic in one sentence	
	Recalls events in proper order	
	Retells text accurately	

Notes :

STUDENT :

AFTER READING	Makes predictions	
	Notices new words	
	Recognises sight words	
	Scans text for clues	
	Scans images for clues	
DURING READING	Applies strategies for new words	
	Reads fluently	
	Self-corrects	
	Re-reads for meaning	
BEFORE READING	Identifies main ideas	
	Summarizes topic in one sentence	
	Recalls events in proper order	
	Retells text accurately	

Notes :

STUDENT :

AFTER READING	Makes predictions	
	Notices new words	
	Recognises sight words	
	Scans text for clues	
	Scans images for clues	
DURING READING	Applies strategies for new words	
	Reads fluently	
	Self-corrects	
	Re-reads for meaning	
BEFORE READING	Identifies main ideas	
	Summarizes topic in one sentence	
	Recalls events in proper order	
	Retells text accurately	

Notes :

STUDENT :

AFTER READING	Makes predictions	
	Notices new words	
	Recognises sight words	
	Scans text for clues	
	Scans images for clues	
DURING READING	Applies strategies for new words	
	Reads fluently	
	Self-corrects	
	Re-reads for meaning	
BEFORE READING	Identifies main ideas	
	Summarizes topic in one sentence	
	Recalls events in proper order	
	Retells text accurately	

Notes :

GUIDED READING PLANBOOK

GROUP :   DATE :

BOOK TITLE :   LEVEL :

✎ BOOK INTRODUCTION :

✎ WORD WORK :   ✎ VOCABULARY :

✎ TEACHING POINT / STRATEGY :

✎ BEFORE READING :

✎ DURING READING :

✎ AFTER READING :

✎ NOTES :

GUIDED READING OBSERVATION NOTES

STUDENT :

AFTER READING
Makes predictions	
Notices new words	
Recognises sight words	
Scans text for clues	
Scans images for clues	

DURING READING
Applies strategies for new words	
Reads fluently	
Self-corrects	
Re-reads for meaning	

BEFORE READING
Identifies main ideas	
Summarizes topic in one sentence	
Recalls events in proper order	
Retells text accurately	

Notes :

STUDENT :

AFTER READING
Makes predictions	
Notices new words	
Recognises sight words	
Scans text for clues	
Scans images for clues	

DURING READING
Applies strategies for new words	
Reads fluently	
Self-corrects	
Re-reads for meaning	

BEFORE READING
Identifies main ideas	
Summarizes topic in one sentence	
Recalls events in proper order	
Retells text accurately	

Notes :

STUDENT :

AFTER READING
Makes predictions	
Notices new words	
Recognises sight words	
Scans text for clues	
Scans images for clues	

DURING READING
Applies strategies for new words	
Reads fluently	
Self-corrects	
Re-reads for meaning	

BEFORE READING
Identifies main ideas	
Summarizes topic in one sentence	
Recalls events in proper order	
Retells text accurately	

Notes :

STUDENT :

AFTER READING
Makes predictions	
Notices new words	
Recognises sight words	
Scans text for clues	
Scans images for clues	

DURING READING
Applies strategies for new words	
Reads fluently	
Self-corrects	
Re-reads for meaning	

BEFORE READING
Identifies main ideas	
Summarizes topic in one sentence	
Recalls events in proper order	
Retells text accurately	

Notes :

STUDENT :

AFTER READING
Makes predictions	
Notices new words	
Recognises sight words	
Scans text for clues	
Scans images for clues	

DURING READING
Applies strategies for new words	
Reads fluently	
Self-corrects	
Re-reads for meaning	

BEFORE READING
Identifies main ideas	
Summarizes topic in one sentence	
Recalls events in proper order	
Retells text accurately	

Notes :

STUDENT :

AFTER READING
Makes predictions	
Notices new words	
Recognises sight words	
Scans text for clues	
Scans images for clues	

DURING READING
Applies strategies for new words	
Reads fluently	
Self-corrects	
Re-reads for meaning	

BEFORE READING
Identifies main ideas	
Summarizes topic in one sentence	
Recalls events in proper order	
Retells text accurately	

Notes :

GUIDED READING PLANBOOK

GROUP : DATE :

BOOK TITLE : LEVEL :

✏ BOOK INTRODUCTION :

✏ WORD WORK :

✏ VOCABULARY :

✏ TEACHING POINT / STRATEGY :

✏ BEFORE READING :

✏ DURING READING :

✏ AFTER READING :

✏ NOTES :

GUIDED READING OBSERVATION NOTES

STUDENT :

AFTER READING	Makes predictions	
	Notices new words	
	Recognises sight words	
	Scans text for clues	
	Scans images for clues	
DURING READING	Applies strategies for new words	
	Reads fluently	
	Self-corrects	
	Re-reads for meaning	
BEFORE READING	Identifies main ideas	
	Summarizes topic in one sentence	
	Recalls events in proper order	
	Retells text accurately	

Notes :

STUDENT :

AFTER READING	Makes predictions	
	Notices new words	
	Recognises sight words	
	Scans text for clues	
	Scans images for clues	
DURING READING	Applies strategies for new words	
	Reads fluently	
	Self-corrects	
	Re-reads for meaning	
BEFORE READING	Identifies main ideas	
	Summarizes topic in one sentence	
	Recalls events in proper order	
	Retells text accurately	

Notes :

STUDENT :

AFTER READING	Makes predictions	
	Notices new words	
	Recognises sight words	
	Scans text for clues	
	Scans images for clues	
DURING READING	Applies strategies for new words	
	Reads fluently	
	Self-corrects	
	Re-reads for meaning	
BEFORE READING	Identifies main ideas	
	Summarizes topic in one sentence	
	Recalls events in proper order	
	Retells text accurately	

Notes :

STUDENT :

AFTER READING	Makes predictions	
	Notices new words	
	Recognises sight words	
	Scans text for clues	
	Scans images for clues	
DURING READING	Applies strategies for new words	
	Reads fluently	
	Self-corrects	
	Re-reads for meaning	
BEFORE READING	Identifies main ideas	
	Summarizes topic in one sentence	
	Recalls events in proper order	
	Retells text accurately	

Notes :

STUDENT :

AFTER READING	Makes predictions	
	Notices new words	
	Recognises sight words	
	Scans text for clues	
	Scans images for clues	
DURING READING	Applies strategies for new words	
	Reads fluently	
	Self-corrects	
	Re-reads for meaning	
BEFORE READING	Identifies main ideas	
	Summarizes topic in one sentence	
	Recalls events in proper order	
	Retells text accurately	

Notes :

STUDENT :

AFTER READING	Makes predictions	
	Notices new words	
	Recognises sight words	
	Scans text for clues	
	Scans images for clues	
DURING READING	Applies strategies for new words	
	Reads fluently	
	Self-corrects	
	Re-reads for meaning	
BEFORE READING	Identifies main ideas	
	Summarizes topic in one sentence	
	Recalls events in proper order	
	Retells text accurately	

Notes :

GUIDED READING PLANBOOK

GROUP :

BOOK TITLE :

DATE :

LEVEL :

✏ BOOK INTRODUCTION :

✏ WORD WORK :

✏ VOCABULARY :

✏ TEACHING POINT / STRATEGY :

✏ BEFORE READING :

✏ DURING READING :

✏ AFTER READING :

✏ NOTES :

GUIDED READING OBSERVATION NOTES

	STUDENT :	
AFTER READING	Makes predictions	
	Notices new words	
	Recognises sight words	
	Scans text for clues	
	Scans images for clues	
DURING READING	Applies strategies for new words	
	Reads fluently	
	Self-corrects	
	Re-reads for meaning	
BEFORE READING	Identifies main ideas	
	Summarizes topic in one sentence	
	Recalls events in proper order	
	Retells text accurately	

Notes :

	STUDENT :	
AFTER READING	Makes predictions	
	Notices new words	
	Recognises sight words	
	Scans text for clues	
	Scans images for clues	
DURING READING	Applies strategies for new words	
	Reads fluently	
	Self-corrects	
	Re-reads for meaning	
BEFORE READING	Identifies main ideas	
	Summarizes topic in one sentence	
	Recalls events in proper order	
	Retells text accurately	

Notes :

	STUDENT :	
AFTER READING	Makes predictions	
	Notices new words	
	Recognises sight words	
	Scans text for clues	
	Scans images for clues	
DURING READING	Applies strategies for new words	
	Reads fluently	
	Self-corrects	
	Re-reads for meaning	
BEFORE READING	Identifies main ideas	
	Summarizes topic in one sentence	
	Recalls events in proper order	
	Retells text accurately	

Notes :

	STUDENT :	
AFTER READING	Makes predictions	
	Notices new words	
	Recognises sight words	
	Scans text for clues	
	Scans images for clues	
DURING READING	Applies strategies for new words	
	Reads fluently	
	Self-corrects	
	Re-reads for meaning	
BEFORE READING	Identifies main ideas	
	Summarizes topic in one sentence	
	Recalls events in proper order	
	Retells text accurately	

Notes :

	STUDENT :	
AFTER READING	Makes predictions	
	Notices new words	
	Recognises sight words	
	Scans text for clues	
	Scans images for clues	
DURING READING	Applies strategies for new words	
	Reads fluently	
	Self-corrects	
	Re-reads for meaning	
BEFORE READING	Identifies main ideas	
	Summarizes topic in one sentence	
	Recalls events in proper order	
	Retells text accurately	

Notes :

	STUDENT :	
AFTER READING	Makes predictions	
	Notices new words	
	Recognises sight words	
	Scans text for clues	
	Scans images for clues	
DURING READING	Applies strategies for new words	
	Reads fluently	
	Self-corrects	
	Re-reads for meaning	
BEFORE READING	Identifies main ideas	
	Summarizes topic in one sentence	
	Recalls events in proper order	
	Retells text accurately	

Notes :

GUIDED READING PLANBOOK

GROUP :   DATE :

BOOK TITLE :   LEVEL :

✏ BOOK INTRODUCTION :

✏ WORD WORK :   ✏ VOCABULARY :

✏ TEACHING POINT / STRATEGY :

✏ BEFORE READING :

✏ DURING READING :

✏ AFTER READING :

✏ NOTES :

GUIDED READING OBSERVATION NOTES

STUDENT :		
AFTER READING	Makes predictions	
	Notices new words	
	Recognises sight words	
	Scans text for clues	
	Scans images for clues	
DURING READING	Applies strategies for new words	
	Reads fluently	
	Self-corrects	
	Re-reads for meaning	
BEFORE READING	Identifies main ideas	
	Summarizes topic in one sentence	
	Recalls events in proper order	
	Retells text accurately	

Notes :

STUDENT :		
AFTER READING	Makes predictions	
	Notices new words	
	Recognises sight words	
	Scans text for clues	
	Scans images for clues	
DURING READING	Applies strategies for new words	
	Reads fluently	
	Self-corrects	
	Re-reads for meaning	
BEFORE READING	Identifies main ideas	
	Summarizes topic in one sentence	
	Recalls events in proper order	
	Retells text accurately	

Notes :

STUDENT :		
AFTER READING	Makes predictions	
	Notices new words	
	Recognises sight words	
	Scans text for clues	
	Scans images for clues	
DURING READING	Applies strategies for new words	
	Reads fluently	
	Self-corrects	
	Re-reads for meaning	
BEFORE READING	Identifies main ideas	
	Summarizes topic in one sentence	
	Recalls events in proper order	
	Retells text accurately	

Notes :

STUDENT :		
AFTER READING	Makes predictions	
	Notices new words	
	Recognises sight words	
	Scans text for clues	
	Scans images for clues	
DURING READING	Applies strategies for new words	
	Reads fluently	
	Self-corrects	
	Re-reads for meaning	
BEFORE READING	Identifies main ideas	
	Summarizes topic in one sentence	
	Recalls events in proper order	
	Retells text accurately	

Notes :

STUDENT :		
AFTER READING	Makes predictions	
	Notices new words	
	Recognises sight words	
	Scans text for clues	
	Scans images for clues	
DURING READING	Applies strategies for new words	
	Reads fluently	
	Self-corrects	
	Re-reads for meaning	
BEFORE READING	Identifies main ideas	
	Summarizes topic in one sentence	
	Recalls events in proper order	
	Retells text accurately	

Notes :

STUDENT :		
AFTER READING	Makes predictions	
	Notices new words	
	Recognises sight words	
	Scans text for clues	
	Scans images for clues	
DURING READING	Applies strategies for new words	
	Reads fluently	
	Self-corrects	
	Re-reads for meaning	
BEFORE READING	Identifies main ideas	
	Summarizes topic in one sentence	
	Recalls events in proper order	
	Retells text accurately	

Notes :

GUIDED READING PLANBOOK

GROUP :   DATE :

BOOK TITLE :   LEVEL :

✏ BOOK INTRODUCTION :

✏ WORD WORK :   ✏ VOCABULARY :

✏ TEACHING POINT / STRATEGY :

✏ BEFORE READING :

✏ DURING READING :

✏ AFTER READING :

✏ NOTES :

GUIDED READING OBSERVATION NOTES

	STUDENT :			STUDENT :			STUDENT :	
AFTER READING	Makes predictions		**AFTER READING**	Makes predictions		**AFTER READING**	Makes predictions	
	Notices new words			Notices new words			Notices new words	
	Recognises sight words			Recognises sight words			Recognises sight words	
	Scans text for clues			Scans text for clues			Scans text for clues	
	Scans images for clues			Scans images for clues			Scans images for clues	
DURING READING	Applies strategies for new words		**DURING READING**	Applies strategies for new words		**DURING READING**	Applies strategies for new words	
	Reads fluently			Reads fluently			Reads fluently	
	Self-corrects			Self-corrects			Self-corrects	
	Re-reads for meaning			Re-reads for meaning			Re-reads for meaning	
BEFORE READING	Identifies main ideas		**BEFORE READING**	Identifies main ideas		**BEFORE READING**	Identifies main ideas	
	Summarizes topic in one sentence			Summarizes topic in one sentence			Summarizes topic in one sentence	
	Recalls events in proper order			Recalls events in proper order			Recalls events in proper order	
	Retells text accurately			Retells text accurately			Retells text accurately	

Notes :   Notes :   Notes :

	STUDENT :			STUDENT :			STUDENT :	
AFTER READING	Makes predictions		**AFTER READING**	Makes predictions		**AFTER READING**	Makes predictions	
	Notices new words			Notices new words			Notices new words	
	Recognises sight words			Recognises sight words			Recognises sight words	
	Scans text for clues			Scans text for clues			Scans text for clues	
	Scans images for clues			Scans images for clues			Scans images for clues	
DURING READING	Applies strategies for new words		**DURING READING**	Applies strategies for new words		**DURING READING**	Applies strategies for new words	
	Reads fluently			Reads fluently			Reads fluently	
	Self-corrects			Self-corrects			Self-corrects	
	Re-reads for meaning			Re-reads for meaning			Re-reads for meaning	
BEFORE READING	Identifies main ideas		**BEFORE READING**	Identifies main ideas		**BEFORE READING**	Identifies main ideas	
	Summarizes topic in one sentence			Summarizes topic in one sentence			Summarizes topic in one sentence	
	Recalls events in proper order			Recalls events in proper order			Recalls events in proper order	
	Retells text accurately			Retells text accurately			Retells text accurately	

Notes :   Notes :   Notes :

GUIDED READING PLANBOOK

GROUP :   DATE :

BOOK TITLE :   LEVEL :

✏ BOOK INTRODUCTION :

✏ WORD WORK :

✏ VOCABULARY :

✏ TEACHING POINT / STRATEGY :

✏ BEFORE READING :

✏ DURING READING :

✏ AFTER READING :

✏ NOTES :

GUIDED READING OBSERVATION NOTES

STUDENT :		
AFTER READING	Makes predictions	
	Notices new words	
	Recognises sight words	
	Scans text for clues	
	Scans images for clues	
DURING READING	Applies strategies for new words	
	Reads fluently	
	Self-corrects	
	Re-reads for meaning	
BEFORE READING	Identifies main ideas	
	Summarizes topic in one sentence	
	Recalls events in proper order	
	Retells text accurately	

Notes :

STUDENT :		
AFTER READING	Makes predictions	
	Notices new words	
	Recognises sight words	
	Scans text for clues	
	Scans images for clues	
DURING READING	Applies strategies for new words	
	Reads fluently	
	Self-corrects	
	Re-reads for meaning	
BEFORE READING	Identifies main ideas	
	Summarizes topic in one sentence	
	Recalls events in proper order	
	Retells text accurately	

Notes :

STUDENT :		
AFTER READING	Makes predictions	
	Notices new words	
	Recognises sight words	
	Scans text for clues	
	Scans images for clues	
DURING READING	Applies strategies for new words	
	Reads fluently	
	Self-corrects	
	Re-reads for meaning	
BEFORE READING	Identifies main ideas	
	Summarizes topic in one sentence	
	Recalls events in proper order	
	Retells text accurately	

Notes :

STUDENT :		
AFTER READING	Makes predictions	
	Notices new words	
	Recognises sight words	
	Scans text for clues	
	Scans images for clues	
DURING READING	Applies strategies for new words	
	Reads fluently	
	Self-corrects	
	Re-reads for meaning	
BEFORE READING	Identifies main ideas	
	Summarizes topic in one sentence	
	Recalls events in proper order	
	Retells text accurately	

Notes :

STUDENT :		
AFTER READING	Makes predictions	
	Notices new words	
	Recognises sight words	
	Scans text for clues	
	Scans images for clues	
DURING READING	Applies strategies for new words	
	Reads fluently	
	Self-corrects	
	Re-reads for meaning	
BEFORE READING	Identifies main ideas	
	Summarizes topic in one sentence	
	Recalls events in proper order	
	Retells text accurately	

Notes :

STUDENT :		
AFTER READING	Makes predictions	
	Notices new words	
	Recognises sight words	
	Scans text for clues	
	Scans images for clues	
DURING READING	Applies strategies for new words	
	Reads fluently	
	Self-corrects	
	Re-reads for meaning	
BEFORE READING	Identifies main ideas	
	Summarizes topic in one sentence	
	Recalls events in proper order	
	Retells text accurately	

Notes :

GUIDED READING PLANBOOK

GROUP :   DATE :

BOOK TITLE :   LEVEL :

✏ BOOK INTRODUCTION :

✏ WORD WORK :   ✏ VOCABULARY :

✏ TEACHING POINT / STRATEGY :

✏ BEFORE READING :

✏ DURING READING :

✏ AFTER READING :

✏ NOTES :

GUIDED READING OBSERVATION NOTES

STUDENT :		
AFTER READING	Makes predictions	
	Notices new words	
	Recognises sight words	
	Scans text for clues	
	Scans images for clues	
DURING READING	Applies strategies for new words	
	Reads fluently	
	Self-corrects	
	Re-reads for meaning	
BEFORE READING	Identifies main ideas	
	Summarizes topic in one sentence	
	Recalls events in proper order	
	Retells text accurately	

Notes :

STUDENT :		
AFTER READING	Makes predictions	
	Notices new words	
	Recognises sight words	
	Scans text for clues	
	Scans images for clues	
DURING READING	Applies strategies for new words	
	Reads fluently	
	Self-corrects	
	Re-reads for meaning	
BEFORE READING	Identifies main ideas	
	Summarizes topic in one sentence	
	Recalls events in proper order	
	Retells text accurately	

Notes :

STUDENT :		
AFTER READING	Makes predictions	
	Notices new words	
	Recognises sight words	
	Scans text for clues	
	Scans images for clues	
DURING READING	Applies strategies for new words	
	Reads fluently	
	Self-corrects	
	Re-reads for meaning	
BEFORE READING	Identifies main ideas	
	Summarizes topic in one sentence	
	Recalls events in proper order	
	Retells text accurately	

Notes :

STUDENT :		
AFTER READING	Makes predictions	
	Notices new words	
	Recognises sight words	
	Scans text for clues	
	Scans images for clues	
DURING READING	Applies strategies for new words	
	Reads fluently	
	Self-corrects	
	Re-reads for meaning	
BEFORE READING	Identifies main ideas	
	Summarizes topic in one sentence	
	Recalls events in proper order	
	Retells text accurately	

Notes :

STUDENT :		
AFTER READING	Makes predictions	
	Notices new words	
	Recognises sight words	
	Scans text for clues	
	Scans images for clues	
DURING READING	Applies strategies for new words	
	Reads fluently	
	Self-corrects	
	Re-reads for meaning	
BEFORE READING	Identifies main ideas	
	Summarizes topic in one sentence	
	Recalls events in proper order	
	Retells text accurately	

Notes :

STUDENT :		
AFTER READING	Makes predictions	
	Notices new words	
	Recognises sight words	
	Scans text for clues	
	Scans images for clues	
DURING READING	Applies strategies for new words	
	Reads fluently	
	Self-corrects	
	Re-reads for meaning	
BEFORE READING	Identifies main ideas	
	Summarizes topic in one sentence	
	Recalls events in proper order	
	Retells text accurately	

Notes :

GUIDED READING PLANBOOK

GROUP :   DATE :

BOOK TITLE :   LEVEL :

✏ BOOK INTRODUCTION :

✏ WORD WORK :   ✏ VOCABULARY :

✏ TEACHING POINT / STRATEGY :

✏ BEFORE READING :

✏ DURING READING :

✏ AFTER READING :

✏ NOTES :

GUIDED READING OBSERVATION NOTES

STUDENT :

AFTER READING	Makes predictions	
	Notices new words	
	Recognises sight words	
	Scans text for clues	
	Scans images for clues	
DURING READING	Applies strategies for new words	
	Reads fluently	
	Self-corrects	
	Re-reads for meaning	
BEFORE READING	Identifies main ideas	
	Summarizes topic in one sentence	
	Recalls events in proper order	
	Retells text accurately	

Notes :

STUDENT :

AFTER READING	Makes predictions	
	Notices new words	
	Recognises sight words	
	Scans text for clues	
	Scans images for clues	
DURING READING	Applies strategies for new words	
	Reads fluently	
	Self-corrects	
	Re-reads for meaning	
BEFORE READING	Identifies main ideas	
	Summarizes topic in one sentence	
	Recalls events in proper order	
	Retells text accurately	

Notes :

STUDENT :

AFTER READING	Makes predictions	
	Notices new words	
	Recognises sight words	
	Scans text for clues	
	Scans images for clues	
DURING READING	Applies strategies for new words	
	Reads fluently	
	Self-corrects	
	Re-reads for meaning	
BEFORE READING	Identifies main ideas	
	Summarizes topic in one sentence	
	Recalls events in proper order	
	Retells text accurately	

Notes :

STUDENT :

AFTER READING	Makes predictions	
	Notices new words	
	Recognises sight words	
	Scans text for clues	
	Scans images for clues	
DURING READING	Applies strategies for new words	
	Reads fluently	
	Self-corrects	
	Re-reads for meaning	
BEFORE READING	Identifies main ideas	
	Summarizes topic in one sentence	
	Recalls events in proper order	
	Retells text accurately	

Notes :

STUDENT :

AFTER READING	Makes predictions	
	Notices new words	
	Recognises sight words	
	Scans text for clues	
	Scans images for clues	
DURING READING	Applies strategies for new words	
	Reads fluently	
	Self-corrects	
	Re-reads for meaning	
BEFORE READING	Identifies main ideas	
	Summarizes topic in one sentence	
	Recalls events in proper order	
	Retells text accurately	

Notes :

STUDENT :

AFTER READING	Makes predictions	
	Notices new words	
	Recognises sight words	
	Scans text for clues	
	Scans images for clues	
DURING READING	Applies strategies for new words	
	Reads fluently	
	Self-corrects	
	Re-reads for meaning	
BEFORE READING	Identifies main ideas	
	Summarizes topic in one sentence	
	Recalls events in proper order	
	Retells text accurately	

Notes :

GUIDED READING PLANBOOK

GROUP :

DATE :

BOOK TITLE :

LEVEL :

✏ BOOK INTRODUCTION :

✏ WORD WORK :

✏ VOCABULARY :

✏ TEACHING POINT / STRATEGY :

✏ BEFORE READING :

✏ DURING READING :

✏ AFTER READING :

✏ NOTES :

GUIDED READING OBSERVATION NOTES

STUDENT :

AFTER READING	Makes predictions	
	Notices new words	
	Recognises sight words	
	Scans text for clues	
	Scans images for clues	
DURING READING	Applies strategies for new words	
	Reads fluently	
	Self-corrects	
	Re-reads for meaning	
BEFORE READING	Identifies main ideas	
	Summarizes topic in one sentence	
	Recalls events in proper order	
	Retells text accurately	

Notes :

STUDENT :

AFTER READING	Makes predictions	
	Notices new words	
	Recognises sight words	
	Scans text for clues	
	Scans images for clues	
DURING READING	Applies strategies for new words	
	Reads fluently	
	Self-corrects	
	Re-reads for meaning	
BEFORE READING	Identifies main ideas	
	Summarizes topic in one sentence	
	Recalls events in proper order	
	Retells text accurately	

Notes :

STUDENT :

AFTER READING	Makes predictions	
	Notices new words	
	Recognises sight words	
	Scans text for clues	
	Scans images for clues	
DURING READING	Applies strategies for new words	
	Reads fluently	
	Self-corrects	
	Re-reads for meaning	
BEFORE READING	Identifies main ideas	
	Summarizes topic in one sentence	
	Recalls events in proper order	
	Retells text accurately	

Notes :

STUDENT :

AFTER READING	Makes predictions	
	Notices new words	
	Recognises sight words	
	Scans text for clues	
	Scans images for clues	
DURING READING	Applies strategies for new words	
	Reads fluently	
	Self-corrects	
	Re-reads for meaning	
BEFORE READING	Identifies main ideas	
	Summarizes topic in one sentence	
	Recalls events in proper order	
	Retells text accurately	

Notes :

STUDENT :

AFTER READING	Makes predictions	
	Notices new words	
	Recognises sight words	
	Scans text for clues	
	Scans images for clues	
DURING READING	Applies strategies for new words	
	Reads fluently	
	Self-corrects	
	Re-reads for meaning	
BEFORE READING	Identifies main ideas	
	Summarizes topic in one sentence	
	Recalls events in proper order	
	Retells text accurately	

Notes :

STUDENT :

AFTER READING	Makes predictions	
	Notices new words	
	Recognises sight words	
	Scans text for clues	
	Scans images for clues	
DURING READING	Applies strategies for new words	
	Reads fluently	
	Self-corrects	
	Re-reads for meaning	
BEFORE READING	Identifies main ideas	
	Summarizes topic in one sentence	
	Recalls events in proper order	
	Retells text accurately	

Notes :

GUIDED READING PLANBOOK

GROUP : DATE :

BOOK TITLE : LEVEL :

✏ BOOK INTRODUCTION :

✏ WORD WORK :

✏ VOCABULARY :

✏ TEACHING POINT / STRATEGY :

✏ BEFORE READING :

✏ DURING READING :

✏ AFTER READING :

✏ NOTES :

GUIDED READING OBSERVATION NOTES

STUDENT :		
AFTER READING	Makes predictions	
	Notices new words	
	Recognises sight words	
	Scans text for clues	
	Scans images for clues	
DURING READING	Applies strategies for new words	
	Reads fluently	
	Self-corrects	
	Re-reads for meaning	
BEFORE READING	Identifies main ideas	
	Summarizes topic in one sentence	
	Recalls events in proper order	
	Retells text accurately	

Notes :

STUDENT :		
AFTER READING	Makes predictions	
	Notices new words	
	Recognises sight words	
	Scans text for clues	
	Scans images for clues	
DURING READING	Applies strategies for new words	
	Reads fluently	
	Self-corrects	
	Re-reads for meaning	
BEFORE READING	Identifies main ideas	
	Summarizes topic in one sentence	
	Recalls events in proper order	
	Retells text accurately	

Notes :

STUDENT :		
AFTER READING	Makes predictions	
	Notices new words	
	Recognises sight words	
	Scans text for clues	
	Scans images for clues	
DURING READING	Applies strategies for new words	
	Reads fluently	
	Self-corrects	
	Re-reads for meaning	
BEFORE READING	Identifies main ideas	
	Summarizes topic in one sentence	
	Recalls events in proper order	
	Retells text accurately	

Notes :

STUDENT :		
AFTER READING	Makes predictions	
	Notices new words	
	Recognises sight words	
	Scans text for clues	
	Scans images for clues	
DURING READING	Applies strategies for new words	
	Reads fluently	
	Self-corrects	
	Re-reads for meaning	
BEFORE READING	Identifies main ideas	
	Summarizes topic in one sentence	
	Recalls events in proper order	
	Retells text accurately	

Notes :

STUDENT :		
AFTER READING	Makes predictions	
	Notices new words	
	Recognises sight words	
	Scans text for clues	
	Scans images for clues	
DURING READING	Applies strategies for new words	
	Reads fluently	
	Self-corrects	
	Re-reads for meaning	
BEFORE READING	Identifies main ideas	
	Summarizes topic in one sentence	
	Recalls events in proper order	
	Retells text accurately	

Notes :

STUDENT :		
AFTER READING	Makes predictions	
	Notices new words	
	Recognises sight words	
	Scans text for clues	
	Scans images for clues	
DURING READING	Applies strategies for new words	
	Reads fluently	
	Self-corrects	
	Re-reads for meaning	
BEFORE READING	Identifies main ideas	
	Summarizes topic in one sentence	
	Recalls events in proper order	
	Retells text accurately	

Notes :

GUIDED READING PLANBOOK

GROUP :

DATE :

BOOK TITLE :

LEVEL :

✏ **BOOK INTRODUCTION :**

✏ **WORD WORK :**

✏ **VOCABULARY :**

✏ **TEACHING POINT / STRATEGY :**

✏ **BEFORE READING :**

✏ **DURING READING :**

✏ **AFTER READING :**

✏ **NOTES :**

GUIDED READING OBSERVATION NOTES

STUDENT :		
AFTER READING	Makes predictions	
	Notices new words	
	Recognises sight words	
	Scans text for clues	
	Scans images for clues	
DURING READING	Applies strategies for new words	
	Reads fluently	
	Self-corrects	
	Re-reads for meaning	
BEFORE READING	Identifies main ideas	
	Summarizes topic in one sentence	
	Recalls events in proper order	
	Retells text accurately	

Notes :

STUDENT :		
AFTER READING	Makes predictions	
	Notices new words	
	Recognises sight words	
	Scans text for clues	
	Scans images for clues	
DURING READING	Applies strategies for new words	
	Reads fluently	
	Self-corrects	
	Re-reads for meaning	
BEFORE READING	Identifies main ideas	
	Summarizes topic in one sentence	
	Recalls events in proper order	
	Retells text accurately	

Notes :

STUDENT :		
AFTER READING	Makes predictions	
	Notices new words	
	Recognises sight words	
	Scans text for clues	
	Scans images for clues	
DURING READING	Applies strategies for new words	
	Reads fluently	
	Self-corrects	
	Re-reads for meaning	
BEFORE READING	Identifies main ideas	
	Summarizes topic in one sentence	
	Recalls events in proper order	
	Retells text accurately	

Notes :

STUDENT :		
AFTER READING	Makes predictions	
	Notices new words	
	Recognises sight words	
	Scans text for clues	
	Scans images for clues	
DURING READING	Applies strategies for new words	
	Reads fluently	
	Self-corrects	
	Re-reads for meaning	
BEFORE READING	Identifies main ideas	
	Summarizes topic in one sentence	
	Recalls events in proper order	
	Retells text accurately	

Notes :

STUDENT :		
AFTER READING	Makes predictions	
	Notices new words	
	Recognises sight words	
	Scans text for clues	
	Scans images for clues	
DURING READING	Applies strategies for new words	
	Reads fluently	
	Self-corrects	
	Re-reads for meaning	
BEFORE READING	Identifies main ideas	
	Summarizes topic in one sentence	
	Recalls events in proper order	
	Retells text accurately	

Notes :

STUDENT :		
AFTER READING	Makes predictions	
	Notices new words	
	Recognises sight words	
	Scans text for clues	
	Scans images for clues	
DURING READING	Applies strategies for new words	
	Reads fluently	
	Self-corrects	
	Re-reads for meaning	
BEFORE READING	Identifies main ideas	
	Summarizes topic in one sentence	
	Recalls events in proper order	
	Retells text accurately	

Notes :

GUIDED READING PLANBOOK

GROUP :   DATE :

BOOK TITLE :   LEVEL :

✎ BOOK INTRODUCTION :

✎ WORD WORK :   ✎ VOCABULARY :

✎ TEACHING POINT / STRATEGY :

✎ BEFORE READING :

✎ DURING READING :

✎ AFTER READING :

✎ NOTES :

GUIDED READING OBSERVATION NOTES

STUDENT :

AFTER READING	Makes predictions	
	Notices new words	
	Recognises sight words	
	Scans text for clues	
	Scans images for clues	
DURING READING	Applies strategies for new words	
	Reads fluently	
	Self-corrects	
	Re-reads for meaning	
BEFORE READING	Identifies main ideas	
	Summarizes topic in one sentence	
	Recalls events in proper order	
	Retells text accurately	

Notes :

STUDENT :

AFTER READING	Makes predictions	
	Notices new words	
	Recognises sight words	
	Scans text for clues	
	Scans images for clues	
DURING READING	Applies strategies for new words	
	Reads fluently	
	Self-corrects	
	Re-reads for meaning	
BEFORE READING	Identifies main ideas	
	Summarizes topic in one sentence	
	Recalls events in proper order	
	Retells text accurately	

Notes :

STUDENT :

AFTER READING	Makes predictions	
	Notices new words	
	Recognises sight words	
	Scans text for clues	
	Scans images for clues	
DURING READING	Applies strategies for new words	
	Reads fluently	
	Self-corrects	
	Re-reads for meaning	
BEFORE READING	Identifies main ideas	
	Summarizes topic in one sentence	
	Recalls events in proper order	
	Retells text accurately	

Notes :

STUDENT :

AFTER READING	Makes predictions	
	Notices new words	
	Recognises sight words	
	Scans text for clues	
	Scans images for clues	
DURING READING	Applies strategies for new words	
	Reads fluently	
	Self-corrects	
	Re-reads for meaning	
BEFORE READING	Identifies main ideas	
	Summarizes topic in one sentence	
	Recalls events in proper order	
	Retells text accurately	

Notes :

STUDENT :

AFTER READING	Makes predictions	
	Notices new words	
	Recognises sight words	
	Scans text for clues	
	Scans images for clues	
DURING READING	Applies strategies for new words	
	Reads fluently	
	Self-corrects	
	Re-reads for meaning	
BEFORE READING	Identifies main ideas	
	Summarizes topic in one sentence	
	Recalls events in proper order	
	Retells text accurately	

Notes :

STUDENT :

AFTER READING	Makes predictions	
	Notices new words	
	Recognises sight words	
	Scans text for clues	
	Scans images for clues	
DURING READING	Applies strategies for new words	
	Reads fluently	
	Self-corrects	
	Re-reads for meaning	
BEFORE READING	Identifies main ideas	
	Summarizes topic in one sentence	
	Recalls events in proper order	
	Retells text accurately	

Notes :

GUIDED READING PLANBOOK

GROUP : DATE :

BOOK TITLE : LEVEL :

✎ BOOK INTRODUCTION :

✎ WORD WORK :

✎ VOCABULARY :

✎ TEACHING POINT / STRATEGY :

✎ BEFORE READING :

✎ DURING READING :

✎ AFTER READING :

✎ NOTES :

GUIDED READING OBSERVATION NOTES

STUDENT :		
AFTER READING	Makes predictions	
	Notices new words	
	Recognises sight words	
	Scans text for clues	
	Scans images for clues	
DURING READING	Applies strategies for new words	
	Reads fluently	
	Self-corrects	
	Re-reads for meaning	
BEFORE READING	Identifies main ideas	
	Summarizes topic in one sentence	
	Recalls events in proper order	
	Retells text accurately	

Notes :

STUDENT :		
AFTER READING	Makes predictions	
	Notices new words	
	Recognises sight words	
	Scans text for clues	
	Scans images for clues	
DURING READING	Applies strategies for new words	
	Reads fluently	
	Self-corrects	
	Re-reads for meaning	
BEFORE READING	Identifies main ideas	
	Summarizes topic in one sentence	
	Recalls events in proper order	
	Retells text accurately	

Notes :

STUDENT :		
AFTER READING	Makes predictions	
	Notices new words	
	Recognises sight words	
	Scans text for clues	
	Scans images for clues	
DURING READING	Applies strategies for new words	
	Reads fluently	
	Self-corrects	
	Re-reads for meaning	
BEFORE READING	Identifies main ideas	
	Summarizes topic in one sentence	
	Recalls events in proper order	
	Retells text accurately	

Notes :

STUDENT :		
AFTER READING	Makes predictions	
	Notices new words	
	Recognises sight words	
	Scans text for clues	
	Scans images for clues	
DURING READING	Applies strategies for new words	
	Reads fluently	
	Self-corrects	
	Re-reads for meaning	
BEFORE READING	Identifies main ideas	
	Summarizes topic in one sentence	
	Recalls events in proper order	
	Retells text accurately	

Notes :

STUDENT :		
AFTER READING	Makes predictions	
	Notices new words	
	Recognises sight words	
	Scans text for clues	
	Scans images for clues	
DURING READING	Applies strategies for new words	
	Reads fluently	
	Self-corrects	
	Re-reads for meaning	
BEFORE READING	Identifies main ideas	
	Summarizes topic in one sentence	
	Recalls events in proper order	
	Retells text accurately	

Notes :

STUDENT :		
AFTER READING	Makes predictions	
	Notices new words	
	Recognises sight words	
	Scans text for clues	
	Scans images for clues	
DURING READING	Applies strategies for new words	
	Reads fluently	
	Self-corrects	
	Re-reads for meaning	
BEFORE READING	Identifies main ideas	
	Summarizes topic in one sentence	
	Recalls events in proper order	
	Retells text accurately	

Notes :

GUIDED READING PLANBOOK

GROUP :

DATE :

BOOK TITLE :

LEVEL :

✏ BOOK INTRODUCTION :

✏ WORD WORK :

✏ VOCABULARY :

✏ TEACHING POINT / STRATEGY :

✏ BEFORE READING :

✏ DURING READING :

✏ AFTER READING :

✏ NOTES :

GUIDED READING OBSERVATION NOTES

STUDENT :

AFTER READING	Makes predictions	
	Notices new words	
	Recognises sight words	
	Scans text for clues	
	Scans images for clues	
DURING READING	Applies strategies for new words	
	Reads fluently	
	Self-corrects	
	Re-reads for meaning	
BEFORE READING	Identifies main ideas	
	Summarizes topic in one sentence	
	Recalls events in proper order	
	Retells text accurately	

Notes :

STUDENT :

AFTER READING	Makes predictions	
	Notices new words	
	Recognises sight words	
	Scans text for clues	
	Scans images for clues	
DURING READING	Applies strategies for new words	
	Reads fluently	
	Self-corrects	
	Re-reads for meaning	
BEFORE READING	Identifies main ideas	
	Summarizes topic in one sentence	
	Recalls events in proper order	
	Retells text accurately	

Notes :

STUDENT :

AFTER READING	Makes predictions	
	Notices new words	
	Recognises sight words	
	Scans text for clues	
	Scans images for clues	
DURING READING	Applies strategies for new words	
	Reads fluently	
	Self-corrects	
	Re-reads for meaning	
BEFORE READING	Identifies main ideas	
	Summarizes topic in one sentence	
	Recalls events in proper order	
	Retells text accurately	

Notes :

STUDENT :

AFTER READING	Makes predictions	
	Notices new words	
	Recognises sight words	
	Scans text for clues	
	Scans images for clues	
DURING READING	Applies strategies for new words	
	Reads fluently	
	Self-corrects	
	Re-reads for meaning	
BEFORE READING	Identifies main ideas	
	Summarizes topic in one sentence	
	Recalls events in proper order	
	Retells text accurately	

Notes :

STUDENT :

AFTER READING	Makes predictions	
	Notices new words	
	Recognises sight words	
	Scans text for clues	
	Scans images for clues	
DURING READING	Applies strategies for new words	
	Reads fluently	
	Self-corrects	
	Re-reads for meaning	
BEFORE READING	Identifies main ideas	
	Summarizes topic in one sentence	
	Recalls events in proper order	
	Retells text accurately	

Notes :

STUDENT :

AFTER READING	Makes predictions	
	Notices new words	
	Recognises sight words	
	Scans text for clues	
	Scans images for clues	
DURING READING	Applies strategies for new words	
	Reads fluently	
	Self-corrects	
	Re-reads for meaning	
BEFORE READING	Identifies main ideas	
	Summarizes topic in one sentence	
	Recalls events in proper order	
	Retells text accurately	

Notes :

GUIDED READING PLANBOOK

GROUP :   DATE :

BOOK TITLE :   LEVEL :

✏ BOOK INTRODUCTION :

✏ WORD WORK :   ✏ VOCABULARY :

✏ TEACHING POINT / STRATEGY :

✏ BEFORE READING :

✏ DURING READING :

✏ AFTER READING :

✏ NOTES :

GUIDED READING OBSERVATION NOTES

STUDENT :		
AFTER READING	Makes predictions	
	Notices new words	
	Recognises sight words	
	Scans text for clues	
	Scans images for clues	
DURING READING	Applies strategies for new words	
	Reads fluently	
	Self-corrects	
	Re-reads for meaning	
BEFORE READING	Identifies main ideas	
	Summarizes topic in one sentence	
	Recalls events in proper order	
	Retells text accurately	

Notes :

STUDENT :		
AFTER READING	Makes predictions	
	Notices new words	
	Recognises sight words	
	Scans text for clues	
	Scans images for clues	
DURING READING	Applies strategies for new words	
	Reads fluently	
	Self-corrects	
	Re-reads for meaning	
BEFORE READING	Identifies main ideas	
	Summarizes topic in one sentence	
	Recalls events in proper order	
	Retells text accurately	

Notes :

STUDENT :		
AFTER READING	Makes predictions	
	Notices new words	
	Recognises sight words	
	Scans text for clues	
	Scans images for clues	
DURING READING	Applies strategies for new words	
	Reads fluently	
	Self-corrects	
	Re-reads for meaning	
BEFORE READING	Identifies main ideas	
	Summarizes topic in one sentence	
	Recalls events in proper order	
	Retells text accurately	

Notes :

STUDENT :		
AFTER READING	Makes predictions	
	Notices new words	
	Recognises sight words	
	Scans text for clues	
	Scans images for clues	
DURING READING	Applies strategies for new words	
	Reads fluently	
	Self-corrects	
	Re-reads for meaning	
BEFORE READING	Identifies main ideas	
	Summarizes topic in one sentence	
	Recalls events in proper order	
	Retells text accurately	

Notes :

STUDENT :		
AFTER READING	Makes predictions	
	Notices new words	
	Recognises sight words	
	Scans text for clues	
	Scans images for clues	
DURING READING	Applies strategies for new words	
	Reads fluently	
	Self-corrects	
	Re-reads for meaning	
BEFORE READING	Identifies main ideas	
	Summarizes topic in one sentence	
	Recalls events in proper order	
	Retells text accurately	

Notes :

STUDENT :		
AFTER READING	Makes predictions	
	Notices new words	
	Recognises sight words	
	Scans text for clues	
	Scans images for clues	
DURING READING	Applies strategies for new words	
	Reads fluently	
	Self-corrects	
	Re-reads for meaning	
BEFORE READING	Identifies main ideas	
	Summarizes topic in one sentence	
	Recalls events in proper order	
	Retells text accurately	

Notes :

GUIDED READING PLANBOOK

GROUP : DATE :

BOOK TITLE : LEVEL :

✏ BOOK INTRODUCTION :

✏ WORD WORK :

✏ VOCABULARY :

✏ TEACHING POINT / STRATEGY :

✏ BEFORE READING :

✏ DURING READING :

✏ AFTER READING :

✏ NOTES :

GUIDED READING OBSERVATION NOTES

	STUDENT :			STUDENT :			STUDENT :	
AFTER READING	Makes predictions		**AFTER READING**	Makes predictions		**AFTER READING**	Makes predictions	
	Notices new words			Notices new words			Notices new words	
	Recognises sight words			Recognises sight words			Recognises sight words	
	Scans text for clues			Scans text for clues			Scans text for clues	
	Scans images for clues			Scans images for clues			Scans images for clues	
DURING READING	Applies strategies for new words		**DURING READING**	Applies strategies for new words		**DURING READING**	Applies strategies for new words	
	Reads fluently			Reads fluently			Reads fluently	
	Self-corrects			Self-corrects			Self-corrects	
	Re-reads for meaning			Re-reads for meaning			Re-reads for meaning	
BEFORE READING	Identifies main ideas		**BEFORE READING**	Identifies main ideas		**BEFORE READING**	Identifies main ideas	
	Summarizes topic in one sentence			Summarizes topic in one sentence			Summarizes topic in one sentence	
	Recalls events in proper order			Recalls events in proper order			Recalls events in proper order	
	Retells text accurately			Retells text accurately			Retells text accurately	

Notes :

	STUDENT :			STUDENT :			STUDENT :	
AFTER READING	Makes predictions		**AFTER READING**	Makes predictions		**AFTER READING**	Makes predictions	
	Notices new words			Notices new words			Notices new words	
	Recognises sight words			Recognises sight words			Recognises sight words	
	Scans text for clues			Scans text for clues			Scans text for clues	
	Scans images for clues			Scans images for clues			Scans images for clues	
DURING READING	Applies strategies for new words		**DURING READING**	Applies strategies for new words		**DURING READING**	Applies strategies for new words	
	Reads fluently			Reads fluently			Reads fluently	
	Self-corrects			Self-corrects			Self-corrects	
	Re-reads for meaning			Re-reads for meaning			Re-reads for meaning	
BEFORE READING	Identifies main ideas		**BEFORE READING**	Identifies main ideas		**BEFORE READING**	Identifies main ideas	
	Summarizes topic in one sentence			Summarizes topic in one sentence			Summarizes topic in one sentence	
	Recalls events in proper order			Recalls events in proper order			Recalls events in proper order	
	Retells text accurately			Retells text accurately			Retells text accurately	

Notes :

GUIDED READING PLANBOOK

GROUP :

DATE :

BOOK TITLE :

LEVEL :

✏ BOOK INTRODUCTION :

✏ WORD WORK :

✏ VOCABULARY :

✏ TEACHING POINT / STRATEGY :

✏ BEFORE READING :

✏ DURING READING :

✏ AFTER READING :

✏ NOTES :

GUIDED READING OBSERVATION NOTES

STUDENT :

AFTER READING
Makes predictions	
Notices new words	
Recognises sight words	
Scans text for clues	
Scans images for clues	

DURING READING
Applies strategies for new words	
Reads fluently	
Self-corrects	
Re-reads for meaning	

BEFORE READING
Identifies main ideas	
Summarizes topic in one sentence	
Recalls events in proper order	
Retells text accurately	

Notes :

STUDENT :

AFTER READING
Makes predictions	
Notices new words	
Recognises sight words	
Scans text for clues	
Scans images for clues	

DURING READING
Applies strategies for new words	
Reads fluently	
Self-corrects	
Re-reads for meaning	

BEFORE READING
Identifies main ideas	
Summarizes topic in one sentence	
Recalls events in proper order	
Retells text accurately	

Notes :

STUDENT :

AFTER READING
Makes predictions	
Notices new words	
Recognises sight words	
Scans text for clues	
Scans images for clues	

DURING READING
Applies strategies for new words	
Reads fluently	
Self-corrects	
Re-reads for meaning	

BEFORE READING
Identifies main ideas	
Summarizes topic in one sentence	
Recalls events in proper order	
Retells text accurately	

Notes :

STUDENT :

AFTER READING
Makes predictions	
Notices new words	
Recognises sight words	
Scans text for clues	
Scans images for clues	

DURING READING
Applies strategies for new words	
Reads fluently	
Self-corrects	
Re-reads for meaning	

BEFORE READING
Identifies main ideas	
Summarizes topic in one sentence	
Recalls events in proper order	
Retells text accurately	

Notes :

STUDENT :

AFTER READING
Makes predictions	
Notices new words	
Recognises sight words	
Scans text for clues	
Scans images for clues	

DURING READING
Applies strategies for new words	
Reads fluently	
Self-corrects	
Re-reads for meaning	

BEFORE READING
Identifies main ideas	
Summarizes topic in one sentence	
Recalls events in proper order	
Retells text accurately	

Notes :

STUDENT :

AFTER READING
Makes predictions	
Notices new words	
Recognises sight words	
Scans text for clues	
Scans images for clues	

DURING READING
Applies strategies for new words	
Reads fluently	
Self-corrects	
Re-reads for meaning	

BEFORE READING
Identifies main ideas	
Summarizes topic in one sentence	
Recalls events in proper order	
Retells text accurately	

Notes :

GUIDED READING PLANBOOK

GROUP :

DATE :

BOOK TITLE :

LEVEL :

✏ BOOK INTRODUCTION :

✏ WORD WORK :

✏ VOCABULARY :

✏ TEACHING POINT / STRATEGY :

✏ BEFORE READING :

✏ DURING READING :

✏ AFTER READING :

✏ NOTES :

GUIDED READING OBSERVATION NOTES

STUDENT :

AFTER READING	Makes predictions	
	Notices new words	
	Recognises sight words	
	Scans text for clues	
	Scans images for clues	
DURING READING	Applies strategies for new words	
	Reads fluently	
	Self-corrects	
	Re-reads for meaning	
BEFORE READING	Identifies main ideas	
	Summarizes topic in one sentence	
	Recalls events in proper order	
	Retells text accurately	

Notes :

STUDENT :

AFTER READING	Makes predictions	
	Notices new words	
	Recognises sight words	
	Scans text for clues	
	Scans images for clues	
DURING READING	Applies strategies for new words	
	Reads fluently	
	Self-corrects	
	Re-reads for meaning	
BEFORE READING	Identifies main ideas	
	Summarizes topic in one sentence	
	Recalls events in proper order	
	Retells text accurately	

Notes :

STUDENT :

AFTER READING	Makes predictions	
	Notices new words	
	Recognises sight words	
	Scans text for clues	
	Scans images for clues	
DURING READING	Applies strategies for new words	
	Reads fluently	
	Self-corrects	
	Re-reads for meaning	
BEFORE READING	Identifies main ideas	
	Summarizes topic in one sentence	
	Recalls events in proper order	
	Retells text accurately	

Notes :

STUDENT :

AFTER READING	Makes predictions	
	Notices new words	
	Recognises sight words	
	Scans text for clues	
	Scans images for clues	
DURING READING	Applies strategies for new words	
	Reads fluently	
	Self-corrects	
	Re-reads for meaning	
BEFORE READING	Identifies main ideas	
	Summarizes topic in one sentence	
	Recalls events in proper order	
	Retells text accurately	

Notes :

STUDENT :

AFTER READING	Makes predictions	
	Notices new words	
	Recognises sight words	
	Scans text for clues	
	Scans images for clues	
DURING READING	Applies strategies for new words	
	Reads fluently	
	Self-corrects	
	Re-reads for meaning	
BEFORE READING	Identifies main ideas	
	Summarizes topic in one sentence	
	Recalls events in proper order	
	Retells text accurately	

Notes :

STUDENT :

AFTER READING	Makes predictions	
	Notices new words	
	Recognises sight words	
	Scans text for clues	
	Scans images for clues	
DURING READING	Applies strategies for new words	
	Reads fluently	
	Self-corrects	
	Re-reads for meaning	
BEFORE READING	Identifies main ideas	
	Summarizes topic in one sentence	
	Recalls events in proper order	
	Retells text accurately	

Notes :

GUIDED READING PLANBOOK

GROUP : DATE :

BOOK TITLE : LEVEL :

✎ BOOK INTRODUCTION :

✎ WORD WORK :

✎ VOCABULARY :

✎ TEACHING POINT / STRATEGY :

✎ BEFORE READING :

✎ DURING READING :

✎ AFTER READING :

✎ NOTES :

GUIDED READING OBSERVATION NOTES

STUDENT :

AFTER READING
Makes predictions	
Notices new words	
Recognises sight words	
Scans text for clues	
Scans images for clues	

DURING READING
Applies strategies for new words	
Reads fluently	
Self-corrects	
Re-reads for meaning	

BEFORE READING
Identifies main ideas	
Summarizes topic in one sentence	
Recalls events in proper order	
Retells text accurately	

Notes :

STUDENT :

AFTER READING
Makes predictions	
Notices new words	
Recognises sight words	
Scans text for clues	
Scans images for clues	

DURING READING
Applies strategies for new words	
Reads fluently	
Self-corrects	
Re-reads for meaning	

BEFORE READING
Identifies main ideas	
Summarizes topic in one sentence	
Recalls events in proper order	
Retells text accurately	

Notes :

STUDENT :

AFTER READING
Makes predictions	
Notices new words	
Recognises sight words	
Scans text for clues	
Scans images for clues	

DURING READING
Applies strategies for new words	
Reads fluently	
Self-corrects	
Re-reads for meaning	

BEFORE READING
Identifies main ideas	
Summarizes topic in one sentence	
Recalls events in proper order	
Retells text accurately	

Notes :

STUDENT :

AFTER READING
Makes predictions	
Notices new words	
Recognises sight words	
Scans text for clues	
Scans images for clues	

DURING READING
Applies strategies for new words	
Reads fluently	
Self-corrects	
Re-reads for meaning	

BEFORE READING
Identifies main ideas	
Summarizes topic in one sentence	
Recalls events in proper order	
Retells text accurately	

Notes :

STUDENT :

AFTER READING
Makes predictions	
Notices new words	
Recognises sight words	
Scans text for clues	
Scans images for clues	

DURING READING
Applies strategies for new words	
Reads fluently	
Self-corrects	
Re-reads for meaning	

BEFORE READING
Identifies main ideas	
Summarizes topic in one sentence	
Recalls events in proper order	
Retells text accurately	

Notes :

STUDENT :

AFTER READING
Makes predictions	
Notices new words	
Recognises sight words	
Scans text for clues	
Scans images for clues	

DURING READING
Applies strategies for new words	
Reads fluently	
Self-corrects	
Re-reads for meaning	

BEFORE READING
Identifies main ideas	
Summarizes topic in one sentence	
Recalls events in proper order	
Retells text accurately	

Notes :

GUIDED READING PLANBOOK

GROUP : DATE :
BOOK TITLE : LEVEL :

✏ BOOK INTRODUCTION :

✏ WORD WORK :   ✏ VOCABULARY :

✏ TEACHING POINT / STRATEGY :

✏ BEFORE READING :

✏ DURING READING :

✏ AFTER READING :

✏ NOTES :

GUIDED READING OBSERVATION NOTES

STUDENT :		
AFTER READING	Makes predictions	
	Notices new words	
	Recognises sight words	
	Scans text for clues	
	Scans images for clues	
DURING READING	Applies strategies for new words	
	Reads fluently	
	Self-corrects	
	Re-reads for meaning	
BEFORE READING	Identifies main ideas	
	Summarizes topic in one sentence	
	Recalls events in proper order	
	Retells text accurately	

Notes :

STUDENT :		
AFTER READING	Makes predictions	
	Notices new words	
	Recognises sight words	
	Scans text for clues	
	Scans images for clues	
DURING READING	Applies strategies for new words	
	Reads fluently	
	Self-corrects	
	Re-reads for meaning	
BEFORE READING	Identifies main ideas	
	Summarizes topic in one sentence	
	Recalls events in proper order	
	Retells text accurately	

Notes :

STUDENT :		
AFTER READING	Makes predictions	
	Notices new words	
	Recognises sight words	
	Scans text for clues	
	Scans images for clues	
DURING READING	Applies strategies for new words	
	Reads fluently	
	Self-corrects	
	Re-reads for meaning	
BEFORE READING	Identifies main ideas	
	Summarizes topic in one sentence	
	Recalls events in proper order	
	Retells text accurately	

Notes :

STUDENT :		
AFTER READING	Makes predictions	
	Notices new words	
	Recognises sight words	
	Scans text for clues	
	Scans images for clues	
DURING READING	Applies strategies for new words	
	Reads fluently	
	Self-corrects	
	Re-reads for meaning	
BEFORE READING	Identifies main ideas	
	Summarizes topic in one sentence	
	Recalls events in proper order	
	Retells text accurately	

Notes :

STUDENT :		
AFTER READING	Makes predictions	
	Notices new words	
	Recognises sight words	
	Scans text for clues	
	Scans images for clues	
DURING READING	Applies strategies for new words	
	Reads fluently	
	Self-corrects	
	Re-reads for meaning	
BEFORE READING	Identifies main ideas	
	Summarizes topic in one sentence	
	Recalls events in proper order	
	Retells text accurately	

Notes :

STUDENT :		
AFTER READING	Makes predictions	
	Notices new words	
	Recognises sight words	
	Scans text for clues	
	Scans images for clues	
DURING READING	Applies strategies for new words	
	Reads fluently	
	Self-corrects	
	Re-reads for meaning	
BEFORE READING	Identifies main ideas	
	Summarizes topic in one sentence	
	Recalls events in proper order	
	Retells text accurately	

Notes :

GUIDED READING PLANBOOK

GROUP :   DATE :

BOOK TITLE :   LEVEL :

✎ BOOK INTRODUCTION :

✎ WORD WORK :   ✎ VOCABULARY :

✎ TEACHING POINT / STRATEGY :

✎ BEFORE READING :

✎ DURING READING :

✎ AFTER READING :

✎ NOTES :

GUIDED READING OBSERVATION NOTES

STUDENT :

AFTER READING	Makes predictions	
	Notices new words	
	Recognises sight words	
	Scans text for clues	
	Scans images for clues	
DURING READING	Applies strategies for new words	
	Reads fluently	
	Self-corrects	
	Re-reads for meaning	
BEFORE READING	Identifies main ideas	
	Summarizes topic in one sentence	
	Recalls events in proper order	
	Retells text accurately	

Notes :

STUDENT :

AFTER READING	Makes predictions	
	Notices new words	
	Recognises sight words	
	Scans text for clues	
	Scans images for clues	
DURING READING	Applies strategies for new words	
	Reads fluently	
	Self-corrects	
	Re-reads for meaning	
BEFORE READING	Identifies main ideas	
	Summarizes topic in one sentence	
	Recalls events in proper order	
	Retells text accurately	

Notes :

STUDENT :

AFTER READING	Makes predictions	
	Notices new words	
	Recognises sight words	
	Scans text for clues	
	Scans images for clues	
DURING READING	Applies strategies for new words	
	Reads fluently	
	Self-corrects	
	Re-reads for meaning	
BEFORE READING	Identifies main ideas	
	Summarizes topic in one sentence	
	Recalls events in proper order	
	Retells text accurately	

Notes :

STUDENT :

AFTER READING	Makes predictions	
	Notices new words	
	Recognises sight words	
	Scans text for clues	
	Scans images for clues	
DURING READING	Applies strategies for new words	
	Reads fluently	
	Self-corrects	
	Re-reads for meaning	
BEFORE READING	Identifies main ideas	
	Summarizes topic in one sentence	
	Recalls events in proper order	
	Retells text accurately	

Notes :

STUDENT :

AFTER READING	Makes predictions	
	Notices new words	
	Recognises sight words	
	Scans text for clues	
	Scans images for clues	
DURING READING	Applies strategies for new words	
	Reads fluently	
	Self-corrects	
	Re-reads for meaning	
BEFORE READING	Identifies main ideas	
	Summarizes topic in one sentence	
	Recalls events in proper order	
	Retells text accurately	

Notes :

STUDENT :

AFTER READING	Makes predictions	
	Notices new words	
	Recognises sight words	
	Scans text for clues	
	Scans images for clues	
DURING READING	Applies strategies for new words	
	Reads fluently	
	Self-corrects	
	Re-reads for meaning	
BEFORE READING	Identifies main ideas	
	Summarizes topic in one sentence	
	Recalls events in proper order	
	Retells text accurately	

Notes :

GUIDED READING PLANBOOK

GROUP :   DATE :

BOOK TITLE :   LEVEL :

✎ **BOOK INTRODUCTION :**

✎ **WORD WORK :**

✎ **VOCABULARY :**

✎ **TEACHING POINT / STRATEGY :**

✎ **BEFORE READING :**

✎ **DURING READING :**

✎ **AFTER READING :**

✎ **NOTES :**

GUIDED READING OBSERVATION NOTES

STUDENT :

AFTER READING	Makes predictions	
	Notices new words	
	Recognises sight words	
	Scans text for clues	
	Scans images for clues	
DURING READING	Applies strategies for new words	
	Reads fluently	
	Self-corrects	
	Re-reads for meaning	
BEFORE READING	Identifies main ideas	
	Summarizes topic in one sentence	
	Recalls events in proper order	
	Retells text accurately	

Notes :

STUDENT :

AFTER READING	Makes predictions	
	Notices new words	
	Recognises sight words	
	Scans text for clues	
	Scans images for clues	
DURING READING	Applies strategies for new words	
	Reads fluently	
	Self-corrects	
	Re-reads for meaning	
BEFORE READING	Identifies main ideas	
	Summarizes topic in one sentence	
	Recalls events in proper order	
	Retells text accurately	

Notes :

STUDENT :

AFTER READING	Makes predictions	
	Notices new words	
	Recognises sight words	
	Scans text for clues	
	Scans images for clues	
DURING READING	Applies strategies for new words	
	Reads fluently	
	Self-corrects	
	Re-reads for meaning	
BEFORE READING	Identifies main ideas	
	Summarizes topic in one sentence	
	Recalls events in proper order	
	Retells text accurately	

Notes :

STUDENT :

AFTER READING	Makes predictions	
	Notices new words	
	Recognises sight words	
	Scans text for clues	
	Scans images for clues	
DURING READING	Applies strategies for new words	
	Reads fluently	
	Self-corrects	
	Re-reads for meaning	
BEFORE READING	Identifies main ideas	
	Summarizes topic in one sentence	
	Recalls events in proper order	
	Retells text accurately	

Notes :

STUDENT :

AFTER READING	Makes predictions	
	Notices new words	
	Recognises sight words	
	Scans text for clues	
	Scans images for clues	
DURING READING	Applies strategies for new words	
	Reads fluently	
	Self-corrects	
	Re-reads for meaning	
BEFORE READING	Identifies main ideas	
	Summarizes topic in one sentence	
	Recalls events in proper order	
	Retells text accurately	

Notes :

STUDENT :

AFTER READING	Makes predictions	
	Notices new words	
	Recognises sight words	
	Scans text for clues	
	Scans images for clues	
DURING READING	Applies strategies for new words	
	Reads fluently	
	Self-corrects	
	Re-reads for meaning	
BEFORE READING	Identifies main ideas	
	Summarizes topic in one sentence	
	Recalls events in proper order	
	Retells text accurately	

Notes :

GUIDED READING PLANBOOK

GROUP : DATE :

BOOK TITLE : LEVEL :

✏ BOOK INTRODUCTION :

✏ WORD WORK :

✏ VOCABULARY :

✏ TEACHING POINT / STRATEGY :

✏ BEFORE READING :

✏ DURING READING :

✏ AFTER READING :

✏ NOTES :

GUIDED READING OBSERVATION NOTES

STUDENT :

AFTER READING
Makes predictions	
Notices new words	
Recognises sight words	
Scans text for clues	
Scans images for clues	

DURING READING
Applies strategies for new words	
Reads fluently	
Self-corrects	
Re-reads for meaning	

BEFORE READING
Identifies main ideas	
Summarizes topic in one sentence	
Recalls events in proper order	
Retells text accurately	

Notes :

STUDENT :

AFTER READING
Makes predictions	
Notices new words	
Recognises sight words	
Scans text for clues	
Scans images for clues	

DURING READING
Applies strategies for new words	
Reads fluently	
Self-corrects	
Re-reads for meaning	

BEFORE READING
Identifies main ideas	
Summarizes topic in one sentence	
Recalls events in proper order	
Retells text accurately	

Notes :

STUDENT :

AFTER READING
Makes predictions	
Notices new words	
Recognises sight words	
Scans text for clues	
Scans images for clues	

DURING READING
Applies strategies for new words	
Reads fluently	
Self-corrects	
Re-reads for meaning	

BEFORE READING
Identifies main ideas	
Summarizes topic in one sentence	
Recalls events in proper order	
Retells text accurately	

Notes :

STUDENT :

AFTER READING
Makes predictions	
Notices new words	
Recognises sight words	
Scans text for clues	
Scans images for clues	

DURING READING
Applies strategies for new words	
Reads fluently	
Self-corrects	
Re-reads for meaning	

BEFORE READING
Identifies main ideas	
Summarizes topic in one sentence	
Recalls events in proper order	
Retells text accurately	

Notes :

STUDENT :

AFTER READING
Makes predictions	
Notices new words	
Recognises sight words	
Scans text for clues	
Scans images for clues	

DURING READING
Applies strategies for new words	
Reads fluently	
Self-corrects	
Re-reads for meaning	

BEFORE READING
Identifies main ideas	
Summarizes topic in one sentence	
Recalls events in proper order	
Retells text accurately	

Notes :

STUDENT :

AFTER READING
Makes predictions	
Notices new words	
Recognises sight words	
Scans text for clues	
Scans images for clues	

DURING READING
Applies strategies for new words	
Reads fluently	
Self-corrects	
Re-reads for meaning	

BEFORE READING
Identifies main ideas	
Summarizes topic in one sentence	
Recalls events in proper order	
Retells text accurately	

Notes :

GUIDED READING PLANBOOK

GROUP :

DATE :

BOOK TITLE :

LEVEL :

✏ BOOK INTRODUCTION :

✏ WORD WORK :

✏ VOCABULARY :

✏ TEACHING POINT / STRATEGY :

✏ BEFORE READING :

✏ DURING READING :

✏ AFTER READING :

✏ NOTES :

GUIDED READING OBSERVATION NOTES

STUDENT :		
AFTER READING	Makes predictions	
	Notices new words	
	Recognises sight words	
	Scans text for clues	
	Scans images for clues	
DURING READING	Applies strategies for new words	
	Reads fluently	
	Self-corrects	
	Re-reads for meaning	
BEFORE READING	Identifies main ideas	
	Summarizes topic in one sentence	
	Recalls events in proper order	
	Retells text accurately	

Notes :

STUDENT :		
AFTER READING	Makes predictions	
	Notices new words	
	Recognises sight words	
	Scans text for clues	
	Scans images for clues	
DURING READING	Applies strategies for new words	
	Reads fluently	
	Self-corrects	
	Re-reads for meaning	
BEFORE READING	Identifies main ideas	
	Summarizes topic in one sentence	
	Recalls events in proper order	
	Retells text accurately	

Notes :

STUDENT :		
AFTER READING	Makes predictions	
	Notices new words	
	Recognises sight words	
	Scans text for clues	
	Scans images for clues	
DURING READING	Applies strategies for new words	
	Reads fluently	
	Self-corrects	
	Re-reads for meaning	
BEFORE READING	Identifies main ideas	
	Summarizes topic in one sentence	
	Recalls events in proper order	
	Retells text accurately	

Notes :

STUDENT :		
AFTER READING	Makes predictions	
	Notices new words	
	Recognises sight words	
	Scans text for clues	
	Scans images for clues	
DURING READING	Applies strategies for new words	
	Reads fluently	
	Self-corrects	
	Re-reads for meaning	
BEFORE READING	Identifies main ideas	
	Summarizes topic in one sentence	
	Recalls events in proper order	
	Retells text accurately	

Notes :

STUDENT :		
AFTER READING	Makes predictions	
	Notices new words	
	Recognises sight words	
	Scans text for clues	
	Scans images for clues	
DURING READING	Applies strategies for new words	
	Reads fluently	
	Self-corrects	
	Re-reads for meaning	
BEFORE READING	Identifies main ideas	
	Summarizes topic in one sentence	
	Recalls events in proper order	
	Retells text accurately	

Notes :

STUDENT :		
AFTER READING	Makes predictions	
	Notices new words	
	Recognises sight words	
	Scans text for clues	
	Scans images for clues	
DURING READING	Applies strategies for new words	
	Reads fluently	
	Self-corrects	
	Re-reads for meaning	
BEFORE READING	Identifies main ideas	
	Summarizes topic in one sentence	
	Recalls events in proper order	
	Retells text accurately	

Notes :

GUIDED READING PLANBOOK

GROUP :

DATE :

BOOK TITLE :

LEVEL :

BOOK INTRODUCTION :

WORD WORK :

VOCABULARY :

TEACHING POINT / STRATEGY :

BEFORE READING :

DURING READING :

AFTER READING :

NOTES :

GUIDED READING OBSERVATION NOTES

STUDENT :

AFTER READING	Makes predictions	
	Notices new words	
	Recognises sight words	
	Scans text for clues	
	Scans images for clues	
DURING READING	Applies strategies for new words	
	Reads fluently	
	Self-corrects	
	Re-reads for meaning	
BEFORE READING	Identifies main ideas	
	Summarizes topic in one sentence	
	Recalls events in proper order	
	Retells text accurately	

Notes :

STUDENT :

AFTER READING	Makes predictions	
	Notices new words	
	Recognises sight words	
	Scans text for clues	
	Scans images for clues	
DURING READING	Applies strategies for new words	
	Reads fluently	
	Self-corrects	
	Re-reads for meaning	
BEFORE READING	Identifies main ideas	
	Summarizes topic in one sentence	
	Recalls events in proper order	
	Retells text accurately	

Notes :

STUDENT :

AFTER READING	Makes predictions	
	Notices new words	
	Recognises sight words	
	Scans text for clues	
	Scans images for clues	
DURING READING	Applies strategies for new words	
	Reads fluently	
	Self-corrects	
	Re-reads for meaning	
BEFORE READING	Identifies main ideas	
	Summarizes topic in one sentence	
	Recalls events in proper order	
	Retells text accurately	

Notes :

STUDENT :

AFTER READING	Makes predictions	
	Notices new words	
	Recognises sight words	
	Scans text for clues	
	Scans images for clues	
DURING READING	Applies strategies for new words	
	Reads fluently	
	Self-corrects	
	Re-reads for meaning	
BEFORE READING	Identifies main ideas	
	Summarizes topic in one sentence	
	Recalls events in proper order	
	Retells text accurately	

Notes :

STUDENT :

AFTER READING	Makes predictions	
	Notices new words	
	Recognises sight words	
	Scans text for clues	
	Scans images for clues	
DURING READING	Applies strategies for new words	
	Reads fluently	
	Self-corrects	
	Re-reads for meaning	
BEFORE READING	Identifies main ideas	
	Summarizes topic in one sentence	
	Recalls events in proper order	
	Retells text accurately	

Notes :

STUDENT :

AFTER READING	Makes predictions	
	Notices new words	
	Recognises sight words	
	Scans text for clues	
	Scans images for clues	
DURING READING	Applies strategies for new words	
	Reads fluently	
	Self-corrects	
	Re-reads for meaning	
BEFORE READING	Identifies main ideas	
	Summarizes topic in one sentence	
	Recalls events in proper order	
	Retells text accurately	

Notes :

GUIDED READING PLANBOOK

GROUP :   DATE :

BOOK TITLE :   LEVEL :

✎ BOOK INTRODUCTION :

✎ WORD WORK :   ✎ VOCABULARY :

✎ TEACHING POINT / STRATEGY :

✎ BEFORE READING :

✎ DURING READING :

✎ AFTER READING :

✎ NOTES :

GUIDED READING OBSERVATION NOTES

STUDENT :

AFTER READING	Makes predictions	
	Notices new words	
	Recognises sight words	
	Scans text for clues	
	Scans images for clues	
DURING READING	Applies strategies for new words	
	Reads fluently	
	Self-corrects	
	Re-reads for meaning	
BEFORE READING	Identifies main ideas	
	Summarizes topic in one sentence	
	Recalls events in proper order	
	Retells text accurately	

Notes :

STUDENT :

AFTER READING	Makes predictions	
	Notices new words	
	Recognises sight words	
	Scans text for clues	
	Scans images for clues	
DURING READING	Applies strategies for new words	
	Reads fluently	
	Self-corrects	
	Re-reads for meaning	
BEFORE READING	Identifies main ideas	
	Summarizes topic in one sentence	
	Recalls events in proper order	
	Retells text accurately	

Notes :

STUDENT :

AFTER READING	Makes predictions	
	Notices new words	
	Recognises sight words	
	Scans text for clues	
	Scans images for clues	
DURING READING	Applies strategies for new words	
	Reads fluently	
	Self-corrects	
	Re-reads for meaning	
BEFORE READING	Identifies main ideas	
	Summarizes topic in one sentence	
	Recalls events in proper order	
	Retells text accurately	

Notes :

STUDENT :

AFTER READING	Makes predictions	
	Notices new words	
	Recognises sight words	
	Scans text for clues	
	Scans images for clues	
DURING READING	Applies strategies for new words	
	Reads fluently	
	Self-corrects	
	Re-reads for meaning	
BEFORE READING	Identifies main ideas	
	Summarizes topic in one sentence	
	Recalls events in proper order	
	Retells text accurately	

Notes :

STUDENT :

AFTER READING	Makes predictions	
	Notices new words	
	Recognises sight words	
	Scans text for clues	
	Scans images for clues	
DURING READING	Applies strategies for new words	
	Reads fluently	
	Self-corrects	
	Re-reads for meaning	
BEFORE READING	Identifies main ideas	
	Summarizes topic in one sentence	
	Recalls events in proper order	
	Retells text accurately	

Notes :

STUDENT :

AFTER READING	Makes predictions	
	Notices new words	
	Recognises sight words	
	Scans text for clues	
	Scans images for clues	
DURING READING	Applies strategies for new words	
	Reads fluently	
	Self-corrects	
	Re-reads for meaning	
BEFORE READING	Identifies main ideas	
	Summarizes topic in one sentence	
	Recalls events in proper order	
	Retells text accurately	

Notes :

GUIDED READING PLANBOOK

GROUP :   DATE :

BOOK TITLE :   LEVEL :

✏ BOOK INTRODUCTION :

✏ WORD WORK :   ✏ VOCABULARY :

✏ TEACHING POINT / STRATEGY :

✏ BEFORE READING :

✏ DURING READING :

✏ AFTER READING :

✏ NOTES :

GUIDED READING OBSERVATION NOTES

STUDENT :		
AFTER READING	Makes predictions	
	Notices new words	
	Recognises sight words	
	Scans text for clues	
	Scans images for clues	
DURING READING	Applies strategies for new words	
	Reads fluently	
	Self-corrects	
	Re-reads for meaning	
BEFORE READING	Identifies main ideas	
	Summarizes topic in one sentence	
	Recalls events in proper order	
	Retells text accurately	

Notes :

STUDENT :		
AFTER READING	Makes predictions	
	Notices new words	
	Recognises sight words	
	Scans text for clues	
	Scans images for clues	
DURING READING	Applies strategies for new words	
	Reads fluently	
	Self-corrects	
	Re-reads for meaning	
BEFORE READING	Identifies main ideas	
	Summarizes topic in one sentence	
	Recalls events in proper order	
	Retells text accurately	

Notes :

STUDENT :		
AFTER READING	Makes predictions	
	Notices new words	
	Recognises sight words	
	Scans text for clues	
	Scans images for clues	
DURING READING	Applies strategies for new words	
	Reads fluently	
	Self-corrects	
	Re-reads for meaning	
BEFORE READING	Identifies main ideas	
	Summarizes topic in one sentence	
	Recalls events in proper order	
	Retells text accurately	

Notes :

STUDENT :		
AFTER READING	Makes predictions	
	Notices new words	
	Recognises sight words	
	Scans text for clues	
	Scans images for clues	
DURING READING	Applies strategies for new words	
	Reads fluently	
	Self-corrects	
	Re-reads for meaning	
BEFORE READING	Identifies main ideas	
	Summarizes topic in one sentence	
	Recalls events in proper order	
	Retells text accurately	

Notes :

STUDENT :		
AFTER READING	Makes predictions	
	Notices new words	
	Recognises sight words	
	Scans text for clues	
	Scans images for clues	
DURING READING	Applies strategies for new words	
	Reads fluently	
	Self-corrects	
	Re-reads for meaning	
BEFORE READING	Identifies main ideas	
	Summarizes topic in one sentence	
	Recalls events in proper order	
	Retells text accurately	

Notes :

STUDENT :		
AFTER READING	Makes predictions	
	Notices new words	
	Recognises sight words	
	Scans text for clues	
	Scans images for clues	
DURING READING	Applies strategies for new words	
	Reads fluently	
	Self-corrects	
	Re-reads for meaning	
BEFORE READING	Identifies main ideas	
	Summarizes topic in one sentence	
	Recalls events in proper order	
	Retells text accurately	

Notes :

GUIDED READING PLANBOOK

GROUP :   DATE :

BOOK TITLE :   LEVEL :

✏ BOOK INTRODUCTION :

✏ WORD WORK :   ✏ VOCABULARY :

✏ TEACHING POINT / STRATEGY :

✏ BEFORE READING :

✏ DURING READING :

✏ AFTER READING :

✏ NOTES :

GUIDED READING OBSERVATION NOTES

STUDENT :

AFTER READING
Makes predictions	
Notices new words	
Recognises sight words	
Scans text for clues	
Scans images for clues	

DURING READING
Applies strategies for new words	
Reads fluently	
Self-corrects	
Re-reads for meaning	

BEFORE READING
Identifies main ideas	
Summarizes topic in one sentence	
Recalls events in proper order	
Retells text accurately	

Notes :

STUDENT :

AFTER READING
Makes predictions	
Notices new words	
Recognises sight words	
Scans text for clues	
Scans images for clues	

DURING READING
Applies strategies for new words	
Reads fluently	
Self-corrects	
Re-reads for meaning	

BEFORE READING
Identifies main ideas	
Summarizes topic in one sentence	
Recalls events in proper order	
Retells text accurately	

Notes :

STUDENT :

AFTER READING
Makes predictions	
Notices new words	
Recognises sight words	
Scans text for clues	
Scans images for clues	

DURING READING
Applies strategies for new words	
Reads fluently	
Self-corrects	
Re-reads for meaning	

BEFORE READING
Identifies main ideas	
Summarizes topic in one sentence	
Recalls events in proper order	
Retells text accurately	

Notes :

STUDENT :

AFTER READING
Makes predictions	
Notices new words	
Recognises sight words	
Scans text for clues	
Scans images for clues	

DURING READING
Applies strategies for new words	
Reads fluently	
Self-corrects	
Re-reads for meaning	

BEFORE READING
Identifies main ideas	
Summarizes topic in one sentence	
Recalls events in proper order	
Retells text accurately	

Notes :

STUDENT :

AFTER READING
Makes predictions	
Notices new words	
Recognises sight words	
Scans text for clues	
Scans images for clues	

DURING READING
Applies strategies for new words	
Reads fluently	
Self-corrects	
Re-reads for meaning	

BEFORE READING
Identifies main ideas	
Summarizes topic in one sentence	
Recalls events in proper order	
Retells text accurately	

Notes :

STUDENT :

AFTER READING
Makes predictions	
Notices new words	
Recognises sight words	
Scans text for clues	
Scans images for clues	

DURING READING
Applies strategies for new words	
Reads fluently	
Self-corrects	
Re-reads for meaning	

BEFORE READING
Identifies main ideas	
Summarizes topic in one sentence	
Recalls events in proper order	
Retells text accurately	

Notes :

GUIDED READING PLANBOOK

GROUP :

DATE :

BOOK TITLE :

LEVEL :

✎ BOOK INTRODUCTION :

✎ WORD WORK :

✎ VOCABULARY :

✎ TEACHING POINT / STRATEGY :

✎ BEFORE READING :

✎ DURING READING :

✎ AFTER READING :

✎ NOTES :

GUIDED READING OBSERVATION NOTES

STUDENT :		
AFTER READING	Makes predictions	
	Notices new words	
	Recognises sight words	
	Scans text for clues	
	Scans images for clues	
DURING READING	Applies strategies for new words	
	Reads fluently	
	Self-corrects	
	Re-reads for meaning	
BEFORE READING	Identifies main ideas	
	Summarizes topic in one sentence	
	Recalls events in proper order	
	Retells text accurately	

Notes :

STUDENT :		
AFTER READING	Makes predictions	
	Notices new words	
	Recognises sight words	
	Scans text for clues	
	Scans images for clues	
DURING READING	Applies strategies for new words	
	Reads fluently	
	Self-corrects	
	Re-reads for meaning	
BEFORE READING	Identifies main ideas	
	Summarizes topic in one sentence	
	Recalls events in proper order	
	Retells text accurately	

Notes :

STUDENT :		
AFTER READING	Makes predictions	
	Notices new words	
	Recognises sight words	
	Scans text for clues	
	Scans images for clues	
DURING READING	Applies strategies for new words	
	Reads fluently	
	Self-corrects	
	Re-reads for meaning	
BEFORE READING	Identifies main ideas	
	Summarizes topic in one sentence	
	Recalls events in proper order	
	Retells text accurately	

Notes :

STUDENT :		
AFTER READING	Makes predictions	
	Notices new words	
	Recognises sight words	
	Scans text for clues	
	Scans images for clues	
DURING READING	Applies strategies for new words	
	Reads fluently	
	Self-corrects	
	Re-reads for meaning	
BEFORE READING	Identifies main ideas	
	Summarizes topic in one sentence	
	Recalls events in proper order	
	Retells text accurately	

Notes :

STUDENT :		
AFTER READING	Makes predictions	
	Notices new words	
	Recognises sight words	
	Scans text for clues	
	Scans images for clues	
DURING READING	Applies strategies for new words	
	Reads fluently	
	Self-corrects	
	Re-reads for meaning	
BEFORE READING	Identifies main ideas	
	Summarizes topic in one sentence	
	Recalls events in proper order	
	Retells text accurately	

Notes :

STUDENT :		
AFTER READING	Makes predictions	
	Notices new words	
	Recognises sight words	
	Scans text for clues	
	Scans images for clues	
DURING READING	Applies strategies for new words	
	Reads fluently	
	Self-corrects	
	Re-reads for meaning	
BEFORE READING	Identifies main ideas	
	Summarizes topic in one sentence	
	Recalls events in proper order	
	Retells text accurately	

Notes :

GUIDED READING PLANBOOK

GROUP :   DATE :

BOOK TITLE :   LEVEL :

✏ BOOK INTRODUCTION :

✏ WORD WORK :

✏ VOCABULARY :

✏ TEACHING POINT / STRATEGY :

✏ BEFORE READING :

✏ DURING READING :

✏ AFTER READING :

✏ NOTES :

GUIDED READING OBSERVATION NOTES

STUDENT :		
AFTER READING	Makes predictions	
	Notices new words	
	Recognises sight words	
	Scans text for clues	
	Scans images for clues	
DURING READING	Applies strategies for new words	
	Reads fluently	
	Self-corrects	
	Re-reads for meaning	
BEFORE READING	Identifies main ideas	
	Summarizes topic in one sentence	
	Recalls events in proper order	
	Retells text accurately	

Notes :

STUDENT :		
AFTER READING	Makes predictions	
	Notices new words	
	Recognises sight words	
	Scans text for clues	
	Scans images for clues	
DURING READING	Applies strategies for new words	
	Reads fluently	
	Self-corrects	
	Re-reads for meaning	
BEFORE READING	Identifies main ideas	
	Summarizes topic in one sentence	
	Recalls events in proper order	
	Retells text accurately	

Notes :

STUDENT :		
AFTER READING	Makes predictions	
	Notices new words	
	Recognises sight words	
	Scans text for clues	
	Scans images for clues	
DURING READING	Applies strategies for new words	
	Reads fluently	
	Self-corrects	
	Re-reads for meaning	
BEFORE READING	Identifies main ideas	
	Summarizes topic in one sentence	
	Recalls events in proper order	
	Retells text accurately	

Notes :

STUDENT :		
AFTER READING	Makes predictions	
	Notices new words	
	Recognises sight words	
	Scans text for clues	
	Scans images for clues	
DURING READING	Applies strategies for new words	
	Reads fluently	
	Self-corrects	
	Re-reads for meaning	
BEFORE READING	Identifies main ideas	
	Summarizes topic in one sentence	
	Recalls events in proper order	
	Retells text accurately	

Notes :

STUDENT :		
AFTER READING	Makes predictions	
	Notices new words	
	Recognises sight words	
	Scans text for clues	
	Scans images for clues	
DURING READING	Applies strategies for new words	
	Reads fluently	
	Self-corrects	
	Re-reads for meaning	
BEFORE READING	Identifies main ideas	
	Summarizes topic in one sentence	
	Recalls events in proper order	
	Retells text accurately	

Notes :

STUDENT :		
AFTER READING	Makes predictions	
	Notices new words	
	Recognises sight words	
	Scans text for clues	
	Scans images for clues	
DURING READING	Applies strategies for new words	
	Reads fluently	
	Self-corrects	
	Re-reads for meaning	
BEFORE READING	Identifies main ideas	
	Summarizes topic in one sentence	
	Recalls events in proper order	
	Retells text accurately	

Notes :

GUIDED READING PLANBOOK

GROUP :   DATE :

BOOK TITLE :   LEVEL :

✏ BOOK INTRODUCTION :

✏ WORD WORK :   ✏ VOCABULARY :

✏ TEACHING POINT / STRATEGY :

✏ BEFORE READING :

✏ DURING READING :

✏ AFTER READING :

✏ NOTES :

GUIDED READING OBSERVATION NOTES

STUDENT:		
AFTER READING	Makes predictions	
	Notices new words	
	Recognises sight words	
	Scans text for clues	
	Scans images for clues	
DURING READING	Applies strategies for new words	
	Reads fluently	
	Self-corrects	
	Re-reads for meaning	
BEFORE READING	Identifies main ideas	
	Summarizes topic in one sentence	
	Recalls events in proper order	
	Retells text accurately	

Notes:

STUDENT:		
AFTER READING	Makes predictions	
	Notices new words	
	Recognises sight words	
	Scans text for clues	
	Scans images for clues	
DURING READING	Applies strategies for new words	
	Reads fluently	
	Self-corrects	
	Re-reads for meaning	
BEFORE READING	Identifies main ideas	
	Summarizes topic in one sentence	
	Recalls events in proper order	
	Retells text accurately	

Notes:

STUDENT:		
AFTER READING	Makes predictions	
	Notices new words	
	Recognises sight words	
	Scans text for clues	
	Scans images for clues	
DURING READING	Applies strategies for new words	
	Reads fluently	
	Self-corrects	
	Re-reads for meaning	
BEFORE READING	Identifies main ideas	
	Summarizes topic in one sentence	
	Recalls events in proper order	
	Retells text accurately	

Notes:

STUDENT:		
AFTER READING	Makes predictions	
	Notices new words	
	Recognises sight words	
	Scans text for clues	
	Scans images for clues	
DURING READING	Applies strategies for new words	
	Reads fluently	
	Self-corrects	
	Re-reads for meaning	
BEFORE READING	Identifies main ideas	
	Summarizes topic in one sentence	
	Recalls events in proper order	
	Retells text accurately	

Notes:

STUDENT:		
AFTER READING	Makes predictions	
	Notices new words	
	Recognises sight words	
	Scans text for clues	
	Scans images for clues	
DURING READING	Applies strategies for new words	
	Reads fluently	
	Self-corrects	
	Re-reads for meaning	
BEFORE READING	Identifies main ideas	
	Summarizes topic in one sentence	
	Recalls events in proper order	
	Retells text accurately	

Notes:

STUDENT:		
AFTER READING	Makes predictions	
	Notices new words	
	Recognises sight words	
	Scans text for clues	
	Scans images for clues	
DURING READING	Applies strategies for new words	
	Reads fluently	
	Self-corrects	
	Re-reads for meaning	
BEFORE READING	Identifies main ideas	
	Summarizes topic in one sentence	
	Recalls events in proper order	
	Retells text accurately	

Notes:

GUIDED READING PLANBOOK

GROUP :   DATE :

BOOK TITLE :   LEVEL :

BOOK INTRODUCTION :

WORD WORK :   **VOCABULARY :**

TEACHING POINT / STRATEGY :

BEFORE READING :

DURING READING :

AFTER READING :

NOTES :

GUIDED READING OBSERVATION NOTES

STUDENT :

AFTER READING	Makes predictions	
	Notices new words	
	Recognises sight words	
	Scans text for clues	
	Scans images for clues	
DURING READING	Applies strategies for new words	
	Reads fluently	
	Self-corrects	
	Re-reads for meaning	
BEFORE READING	Identifies main ideas	
	Summarizes topic in one sentence	
	Recalls events in proper order	
	Retells text accurately	

Notes :

STUDENT :

AFTER READING	Makes predictions	
	Notices new words	
	Recognises sight words	
	Scans text for clues	
	Scans images for clues	
DURING READING	Applies strategies for new words	
	Reads fluently	
	Self-corrects	
	Re-reads for meaning	
BEFORE READING	Identifies main ideas	
	Summarizes topic in one sentence	
	Recalls events in proper order	
	Retells text accurately	

Notes :

STUDENT :

AFTER READING	Makes predictions	
	Notices new words	
	Recognises sight words	
	Scans text for clues	
	Scans images for clues	
DURING READING	Applies strategies for new words	
	Reads fluently	
	Self-corrects	
	Re-reads for meaning	
BEFORE READING	Identifies main ideas	
	Summarizes topic in one sentence	
	Recalls events in proper order	
	Retells text accurately	

Notes :

STUDENT :

AFTER READING	Makes predictions	
	Notices new words	
	Recognises sight words	
	Scans text for clues	
	Scans images for clues	
DURING READING	Applies strategies for new words	
	Reads fluently	
	Self-corrects	
	Re-reads for meaning	
BEFORE READING	Identifies main ideas	
	Summarizes topic in one sentence	
	Recalls events in proper order	
	Retells text accurately	

Notes :

STUDENT :

AFTER READING	Makes predictions	
	Notices new words	
	Recognises sight words	
	Scans text for clues	
	Scans images for clues	
DURING READING	Applies strategies for new words	
	Reads fluently	
	Self-corrects	
	Re-reads for meaning	
BEFORE READING	Identifies main ideas	
	Summarizes topic in one sentence	
	Recalls events in proper order	
	Retells text accurately	

Notes :

STUDENT :

AFTER READING	Makes predictions	
	Notices new words	
	Recognises sight words	
	Scans text for clues	
	Scans images for clues	
DURING READING	Applies strategies for new words	
	Reads fluently	
	Self-corrects	
	Re-reads for meaning	
BEFORE READING	Identifies main ideas	
	Summarizes topic in one sentence	
	Recalls events in proper order	
	Retells text accurately	

Notes :

GUIDED READING PLANBOOK

GROUP :   DATE :

BOOK TITLE :   LEVEL :

BOOK INTRODUCTION :

WORD WORK :   **VOCABULARY :**

TEACHING POINT / STRATEGY :

BEFORE READING :

DURING READING :

AFTER READING :

NOTES :

GUIDED READING OBSERVATION NOTES

	STUDENT :	
AFTER READING	Makes predictions	
	Notices new words	
	Recognises sight words	
	Scans text for clues	
	Scans images for clues	
DURING READING	Applies strategies for new words	
	Reads fluently	
	Self-corrects	
	Re-reads for meaning	
BEFORE READING	Identifies main ideas	
	Summarizes topic in one sentence	
	Recalls events in proper order	
	Retells text accurately	

Notes :

	STUDENT :	
AFTER READING	Makes predictions	
	Notices new words	
	Recognises sight words	
	Scans text for clues	
	Scans images for clues	
DURING READING	Applies strategies for new words	
	Reads fluently	
	Self-corrects	
	Re-reads for meaning	
BEFORE READING	Identifies main ideas	
	Summarizes topic in one sentence	
	Recalls events in proper order	
	Retells text accurately	

Notes :

	STUDENT :	
AFTER READING	Makes predictions	
	Notices new words	
	Recognises sight words	
	Scans text for clues	
	Scans images for clues	
DURING READING	Applies strategies for new words	
	Reads fluently	
	Self-corrects	
	Re-reads for meaning	
BEFORE READING	Identifies main ideas	
	Summarizes topic in one sentence	
	Recalls events in proper order	
	Retells text accurately	

Notes :

	STUDENT :	
AFTER READING	Makes predictions	
	Notices new words	
	Recognises sight words	
	Scans text for clues	
	Scans images for clues	
DURING READING	Applies strategies for new words	
	Reads fluently	
	Self-corrects	
	Re-reads for meaning	
BEFORE READING	Identifies main ideas	
	Summarizes topic in one sentence	
	Recalls events in proper order	
	Retells text accurately	

Notes :

	STUDENT :	
AFTER READING	Makes predictions	
	Notices new words	
	Recognises sight words	
	Scans text for clues	
	Scans images for clues	
DURING READING	Applies strategies for new words	
	Reads fluently	
	Self-corrects	
	Re-reads for meaning	
BEFORE READING	Identifies main ideas	
	Summarizes topic in one sentence	
	Recalls events in proper order	
	Retells text accurately	

Notes :

	STUDENT :	
AFTER READING	Makes predictions	
	Notices new words	
	Recognises sight words	
	Scans text for clues	
	Scans images for clues	
DURING READING	Applies strategies for new words	
	Reads fluently	
	Self-corrects	
	Re-reads for meaning	
BEFORE READING	Identifies main ideas	
	Summarizes topic in one sentence	
	Recalls events in proper order	
	Retells text accurately	

Notes :

GUIDED READING PLANBOOK

GROUP :   DATE :

BOOK TITLE :   LEVEL :

BOOK INTRODUCTION :

WORD WORK :

VOCABULARY :

TEACHING POINT / STRATEGY :

BEFORE READING :

DURING READING :

AFTER READING :

NOTES :

GUIDED READING OBSERVATION NOTES

STUDENT :		
AFTER READING	Makes predictions	
	Notices new words	
	Recognises sight words	
	Scans text for clues	
	Scans images for clues	
DURING READING	Applies strategies for new words	
	Reads fluently	
	Self-corrects	
	Re-reads for meaning	
BEFORE READING	Identifies main ideas	
	Summarizes topic in one sentence	
	Recalls events in proper order	
	Retells text accurately	

Notes :

STUDENT :		
AFTER READING	Makes predictions	
	Notices new words	
	Recognises sight words	
	Scans text for clues	
	Scans images for clues	
DURING READING	Applies strategies for new words	
	Reads fluently	
	Self-corrects	
	Re-reads for meaning	
BEFORE READING	Identifies main ideas	
	Summarizes topic in one sentence	
	Recalls events in proper order	
	Retells text accurately	

Notes :

STUDENT :		
AFTER READING	Makes predictions	
	Notices new words	
	Recognises sight words	
	Scans text for clues	
	Scans images for clues	
DURING READING	Applies strategies for new words	
	Reads fluently	
	Self-corrects	
	Re-reads for meaning	
BEFORE READING	Identifies main ideas	
	Summarizes topic in one sentence	
	Recalls events in proper order	
	Retells text accurately	

Notes :

STUDENT :		
AFTER READING	Makes predictions	
	Notices new words	
	Recognises sight words	
	Scans text for clues	
	Scans images for clues	
DURING READING	Applies strategies for new words	
	Reads fluently	
	Self-corrects	
	Re-reads for meaning	
BEFORE READING	Identifies main ideas	
	Summarizes topic in one sentence	
	Recalls events in proper order	
	Retells text accurately	

Notes :

STUDENT :		
AFTER READING	Makes predictions	
	Notices new words	
	Recognises sight words	
	Scans text for clues	
	Scans images for clues	
DURING READING	Applies strategies for new words	
	Reads fluently	
	Self-corrects	
	Re-reads for meaning	
BEFORE READING	Identifies main ideas	
	Summarizes topic in one sentence	
	Recalls events in proper order	
	Retells text accurately	

Notes :

STUDENT :		
AFTER READING	Makes predictions	
	Notices new words	
	Recognises sight words	
	Scans text for clues	
	Scans images for clues	
DURING READING	Applies strategies for new words	
	Reads fluently	
	Self-corrects	
	Re-reads for meaning	
BEFORE READING	Identifies main ideas	
	Summarizes topic in one sentence	
	Recalls events in proper order	
	Retells text accurately	

Notes :

GUIDED READING PLANBOOK

GROUP :   DATE :

BOOK TITLE :   LEVEL :

✎ BOOK INTRODUCTION :

✎ WORD WORK :

✎ VOCABULARY :

✎ TEACHING POINT / STRATEGY :

✎ BEFORE READING :

✎ DURING READING :

✎ AFTER READING :

✎ NOTES :

GUIDED READING OBSERVATION NOTES

STUDENT :		
AFTER READING	Makes predictions	
	Notices new words	
	Recognises sight words	
	Scans text for clues	
	Scans images for clues	
DURING READING	Applies strategies for new words	
	Reads fluently	
	Self-corrects	
	Re-reads for meaning	
BEFORE READING	Identifies main ideas	
	Summarizes topic in one sentence	
	Recalls events in proper order	
	Retells text accurately	

Notes :

STUDENT :		
AFTER READING	Makes predictions	
	Notices new words	
	Recognises sight words	
	Scans text for clues	
	Scans images for clues	
DURING READING	Applies strategies for new words	
	Reads fluently	
	Self-corrects	
	Re-reads for meaning	
BEFORE READING	Identifies main ideas	
	Summarizes topic in one sentence	
	Recalls events in proper order	
	Retells text accurately	

Notes :

STUDENT :		
AFTER READING	Makes predictions	
	Notices new words	
	Recognises sight words	
	Scans text for clues	
	Scans images for clues	
DURING READING	Applies strategies for new words	
	Reads fluently	
	Self-corrects	
	Re-reads for meaning	
BEFORE READING	Identifies main ideas	
	Summarizes topic in one sentence	
	Recalls events in proper order	
	Retells text accurately	

Notes :

STUDENT :		
AFTER READING	Makes predictions	
	Notices new words	
	Recognises sight words	
	Scans text for clues	
	Scans images for clues	
DURING READING	Applies strategies for new words	
	Reads fluently	
	Self-corrects	
	Re-reads for meaning	
BEFORE READING	Identifies main ideas	
	Summarizes topic in one sentence	
	Recalls events in proper order	
	Retells text accurately	

Notes :

STUDENT :		
AFTER READING	Makes predictions	
	Notices new words	
	Recognises sight words	
	Scans text for clues	
	Scans images for clues	
DURING READING	Applies strategies for new words	
	Reads fluently	
	Self-corrects	
	Re-reads for meaning	
BEFORE READING	Identifies main ideas	
	Summarizes topic in one sentence	
	Recalls events in proper order	
	Retells text accurately	

Notes :

STUDENT :		
AFTER READING	Makes predictions	
	Notices new words	
	Recognises sight words	
	Scans text for clues	
	Scans images for clues	
DURING READING	Applies strategies for new words	
	Reads fluently	
	Self-corrects	
	Re-reads for meaning	
BEFORE READING	Identifies main ideas	
	Summarizes topic in one sentence	
	Recalls events in proper order	
	Retells text accurately	

Notes :

GUIDED READING PLANBOOK

GROUP :   DATE :

BOOK TITLE :   LEVEL :

✏ BOOK INTRODUCTION :

✏ WORD WORK :   ✏ VOCABULARY :

✏ TEACHING POINT / STRATEGY :

✏ BEFORE READING :

✏ DURING READING :

✏ AFTER READING :

✏ NOTES :

GUIDED READING OBSERVATION NOTES

STUDENT :		
AFTER READING	Makes predictions	
	Notices new words	
	Recognises sight words	
	Scans text for clues	
	Scans images for clues	
DURING READING	Applies strategies for new words	
	Reads fluently	
	Self-corrects	
	Re-reads for meaning	
BEFORE READING	Identifies main ideas	
	Summarizes topic in one sentence	
	Recalls events in proper order	
	Retells text accurately	

Notes :

STUDENT :		
AFTER READING	Makes predictions	
	Notices new words	
	Recognises sight words	
	Scans text for clues	
	Scans images for clues	
DURING READING	Applies strategies for new words	
	Reads fluently	
	Self-corrects	
	Re-reads for meaning	
BEFORE READING	Identifies main ideas	
	Summarizes topic in one sentence	
	Recalls events in proper order	
	Retells text accurately	

Notes :

STUDENT :		
AFTER READING	Makes predictions	
	Notices new words	
	Recognises sight words	
	Scans text for clues	
	Scans images for clues	
DURING READING	Applies strategies for new words	
	Reads fluently	
	Self-corrects	
	Re-reads for meaning	
BEFORE READING	Identifies main ideas	
	Summarizes topic in one sentence	
	Recalls events in proper order	
	Retells text accurately	

Notes :

STUDENT :		
AFTER READING	Makes predictions	
	Notices new words	
	Recognises sight words	
	Scans text for clues	
	Scans images for clues	
DURING READING	Applies strategies for new words	
	Reads fluently	
	Self-corrects	
	Re-reads for meaning	
BEFORE READING	Identifies main ideas	
	Summarizes topic in one sentence	
	Recalls events in proper order	
	Retells text accurately	

Notes :

STUDENT :		
AFTER READING	Makes predictions	
	Notices new words	
	Recognises sight words	
	Scans text for clues	
	Scans images for clues	
DURING READING	Applies strategies for new words	
	Reads fluently	
	Self-corrects	
	Re-reads for meaning	
BEFORE READING	Identifies main ideas	
	Summarizes topic in one sentence	
	Recalls events in proper order	
	Retells text accurately	

Notes :

STUDENT :		
AFTER READING	Makes predictions	
	Notices new words	
	Recognises sight words	
	Scans text for clues	
	Scans images for clues	
DURING READING	Applies strategies for new words	
	Reads fluently	
	Self-corrects	
	Re-reads for meaning	
BEFORE READING	Identifies main ideas	
	Summarizes topic in one sentence	
	Recalls events in proper order	
	Retells text accurately	

Notes :

GUIDED READING PLANBOOK

GROUP :
BOOK TITLE :

DATE :
LEVEL :

✏ BOOK INTRODUCTION :

✏ WORD WORK :

✏ VOCABULARY :

✏ TEACHING POINT / STRATEGY :

✏ BEFORE READING :

✏ DURING READING :

✏ AFTER READING :

✏ NOTES :

GUIDED READING OBSERVATION NOTES

	STUDENT :	
AFTER READING	Makes predictions	
	Notices new words	
	Recognises sight words	
	Scans text for clues	
	Scans images for clues	
DURING READING	Applies strategies for new words	
	Reads fluently	
	Self-corrects	
	Re-reads for meaning	
BEFORE READING	Identifies main ideas	
	Summarizes topic in one sentence	
	Recalls events in proper order	
	Retells text accurately	

Notes :

	STUDENT :	
AFTER READING	Makes predictions	
	Notices new words	
	Recognises sight words	
	Scans text for clues	
	Scans images for clues	
DURING READING	Applies strategies for new words	
	Reads fluently	
	Self-corrects	
	Re-reads for meaning	
BEFORE READING	Identifies main ideas	
	Summarizes topic in one sentence	
	Recalls events in proper order	
	Retells text accurately	

Notes :

	STUDENT :	
AFTER READING	Makes predictions	
	Notices new words	
	Recognises sight words	
	Scans text for clues	
	Scans images for clues	
DURING READING	Applies strategies for new words	
	Reads fluently	
	Self-corrects	
	Re-reads for meaning	
BEFORE READING	Identifies main ideas	
	Summarizes topic in one sentence	
	Recalls events in proper order	
	Retells text accurately	

Notes :

	STUDENT :	
AFTER READING	Makes predictions	
	Notices new words	
	Recognises sight words	
	Scans text for clues	
	Scans images for clues	
DURING READING	Applies strategies for new words	
	Reads fluently	
	Self-corrects	
	Re-reads for meaning	
BEFORE READING	Identifies main ideas	
	Summarizes topic in one sentence	
	Recalls events in proper order	
	Retells text accurately	

Notes :

	STUDENT :	
AFTER READING	Makes predictions	
	Notices new words	
	Recognises sight words	
	Scans text for clues	
	Scans images for clues	
DURING READING	Applies strategies for new words	
	Reads fluently	
	Self-corrects	
	Re-reads for meaning	
BEFORE READING	Identifies main ideas	
	Summarizes topic in one sentence	
	Recalls events in proper order	
	Retells text accurately	

Notes :

	STUDENT :	
AFTER READING	Makes predictions	
	Notices new words	
	Recognises sight words	
	Scans text for clues	
	Scans images for clues	
DURING READING	Applies strategies for new words	
	Reads fluently	
	Self-corrects	
	Re-reads for meaning	
BEFORE READING	Identifies main ideas	
	Summarizes topic in one sentence	
	Recalls events in proper order	
	Retells text accurately	

Notes :

GUIDED READING PLANBOOK

GROUP :   DATE :

BOOK TITLE :   LEVEL :

BOOK INTRODUCTION :

WORD WORK :

VOCABULARY :

TEACHING POINT / STRATEGY :

BEFORE READING :

DURING READING :

AFTER READING :

NOTES :

GUIDED READING OBSERVATION NOTES

	STUDENT :	
AFTER READING	Makes predictions	
	Notices new words	
	Recognises sight words	
	Scans text for clues	
	Scans images for clues	
DURING READING	Applies strategies for new words	
	Reads fluently	
	Self-corrects	
	Re-reads for meaning	
BEFORE READING	Identifies main ideas	
	Summarizes topic in one sentence	
	Recalls events in proper order	
	Retells text accurately	

Notes :

	STUDENT :	
AFTER READING	Makes predictions	
	Notices new words	
	Recognises sight words	
	Scans text for clues	
	Scans images for clues	
DURING READING	Applies strategies for new words	
	Reads fluently	
	Self-corrects	
	Re-reads for meaning	
BEFORE READING	Identifies main ideas	
	Summarizes topic in one sentence	
	Recalls events in proper order	
	Retells text accurately	

Notes :

	STUDENT :	
AFTER READING	Makes predictions	
	Notices new words	
	Recognises sight words	
	Scans text for clues	
	Scans images for clues	
DURING READING	Applies strategies for new words	
	Reads fluently	
	Self-corrects	
	Re-reads for meaning	
BEFORE READING	Identifies main ideas	
	Summarizes topic in one sentence	
	Recalls events in proper order	
	Retells text accurately	

Notes :

	STUDENT :	
AFTER READING	Makes predictions	
	Notices new words	
	Recognises sight words	
	Scans text for clues	
	Scans images for clues	
DURING READING	Applies strategies for new words	
	Reads fluently	
	Self-corrects	
	Re-reads for meaning	
BEFORE READING	Identifies main ideas	
	Summarizes topic in one sentence	
	Recalls events in proper order	
	Retells text accurately	

Notes :

	STUDENT :	
AFTER READING	Makes predictions	
	Notices new words	
	Recognises sight words	
	Scans text for clues	
	Scans images for clues	
DURING READING	Applies strategies for new words	
	Reads fluently	
	Self-corrects	
	Re-reads for meaning	
BEFORE READING	Identifies main ideas	
	Summarizes topic in one sentence	
	Recalls events in proper order	
	Retells text accurately	

Notes :

	STUDENT :	
AFTER READING	Makes predictions	
	Notices new words	
	Recognises sight words	
	Scans text for clues	
	Scans images for clues	
DURING READING	Applies strategies for new words	
	Reads fluently	
	Self-corrects	
	Re-reads for meaning	
BEFORE READING	Identifies main ideas	
	Summarizes topic in one sentence	
	Recalls events in proper order	
	Retells text accurately	

Notes :